Guide to
MARTHA'S VINEYARD

GUIDE TO
MARTHA'S VINEYARD

Sixth Edition

by
Polly Burroughs

Photographs by Mike Wallo

A Voyager Book

The Globe Pequot Press

Old Saybrook, Connecticut

Library of Congress Cataloging-in-Publication Data
Burroughs, Polly.
    Guide to Martha's Vineyard / by Polly Burroughs; photographs by Mike Wallo. — 6th ed.
        p.   cm.
    "A Voyager Book"
    Includes index.
    ISBN 1-56440-239-8
    1. Martha's Vineyard (Mass.) — Guidebooks.   I. Title.
F72.M5B875 1993
917.44'94—dc20   93-961
                                                                   CIP

Manufactured in the United States of America
Sixth Edition/Fourth Printing

DO'S AND DON'TS

DO pay attention to the posted rules and regulations at all beaches.

DO use bicycle paths if you are bicycling.

DO have the proper light and reflectors when bicycling at night.

DO watch out for one-way streets in the towns. The streets were laid out in the nineteenth century, and the narrow ones in the center of all three Down-Island towns are one-way.

DO keep your voice down in the towns during the evening hours. No shouting! This has become a serious problem.

DO be responsible for your own trash.

DO keep your dog on a leash at all times when in public, and keep your cat confined to your property out of consideration for others.

DON'T drive on any dunes, or trample them, or harm the vegetation.

DON'T pick any wildflowers.

DON'T disturb any small clams, scallops, or other shellfish.

DON'T bicycle on the sidewalks.

DON'T wear bathing suits in the center of the towns.

DON'T leave any litter on any street, beach, or roadway.

DON'T sleep in your car or on the beach anywhere on the island. It is illegal.

DON'T drive over 45 miles per hour; the speed limit is even slower on most roads.

DON'T dump any boat sewage into the harbors. There is a heavy fine.

CONTENTS

All-Island Map

WEST TISBUR

VINEYARD SOUND

CHILMARK

WEST TISBURY
CENTER

GAY HEAD CLIFFS
AND LIGHTHOUSE

MENEMSHA

GAY HEAD

CHILMARK
CENTER

SOUTH BEACH

ATLANTIC OCEAN

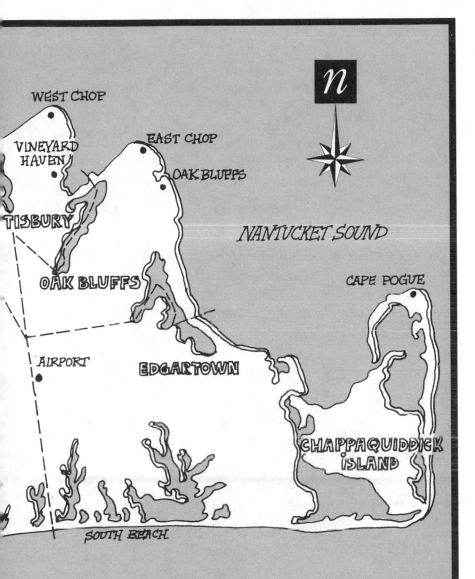

1

THE ISLAND'S PROFILE

The island of Martha's Vineyard lies 5 miles off the shoulder of Cape Cod. Twenty miles long and 9 miles wide at its broadest point, the island is triangular and encircled by the Vineyard Sound, the Nantucket Sound, and the Atlantic Ocean. With hills, valleys, and flat plains, the island is as renowned for the beauty of its varied geological landscape as it is for the individual character of its six towns.

A boulder-strewn ridge runs all along the north shore of the island, extending to the high, rolling moors at the island's western tip. The wooded, mid-island outwash plains, which were formed by the waters that flowed from melting glacial ice, reach down to the windswept beaches along the south shore, where fingerlike ponds jut in from the ocean. Estuaries rich with marine and bird life fringe the island's shores. Four superb harbors are sculpted into the Vineyard and Nantucket Sound side of the island. From the beginning of time, the sea and winds have shaped and reshaped these contours, just as they have helped shape the island's human history since the arrival of the first permanent white settlers in 1642.

Of all the island's assets, the sea and the ocean beaches are the great attraction for vacationers. Once the artery for America's founding and development, and to the Vineyarders their livelihood and only means of communication with the outside world, the sea has once again given the island its economic base by attracting thousands of vacationers each summer. It is an extremely popular summer resort. The number of hotels, inns, and guest houses, restaurants and stores, as well as the variety of concerts, lectures, fairs, sports, walking tours, auctions, performing arts, and other activities for the visitor, has increased dramatically in the past ten years. While the winter population of 14,000 has increased slowly through the years, the summer influx of vacationers quickly escalates to 100,000 by early July, not counting the day-trippers who come over on cruise ships to visit the island or those in hotels and inns.

To cope with the burgeoning number of visitors each summer, certain changes have been made. There are many more ferries running than in the past; shuttle buses serve three of the towns; free parking arrangements have been made to cope with traffic congestion; and many more places to stay, eat, shop, and rent cars and bikes have become available to the public. And yet, not everything has changed, for standards to preserve the scenic beauty of the island continue as they have for years. There are no bathhouses or food stands at any of the beaches; there are still no traffic lights on the island; and signs at many beaches and wildlife sanctuaries warn visitors not to disturb bird nesting areas, trample or drive on the dunes, or leave litter.

Despite the growth of the island population, tradition runs deep in all six towns. Evidence of their Yankee heritage is most apparent in the off-season when the population dwindles. The pace slackens, and islanders settle down to small-town life with its small-town rhythms.

The six towns are as well known for their individuality as were the early Yankees, whose independent character and idiosyncracies are legendary. Certain customs have prevailed, and one is the usage of the terms Up-Island and Down-Island, which are important for the newcomer to understand.

When a ship sails in an easterly direction, it is decreasing or running "down" the degrees of longitude toward zero at Greenwich, England. A westbound vessel, on the other hand, is running "up" its longitude. Thus the Down-Island towns are those on the eastern and northeastern ends of the island: Vineyard Haven, Oak Bluffs, Edgartown, and the island of Chappaquiddick. The Up-Island communities include North and West Tisbury (which are geographically in mid-island, but considered Up-Island), and Chilmark and Gay Head at the westernmost tip. A ship moving through Vineyard Sound sails "up" to New York and "down" east to Maine.

The island's principal port of entry and bustling commercial center is Vineyard Haven, whose maritime origins are rooted in coastal shipping. The town's residential areas have more year-round homes than are found elsewhere on the island. There are some attractive and quiet places to stay a few blocks from the center, and the visitor will find good restaurants, attractive gift shops, and bike, moped, car, and boat rentals readily available. Although the town does have two small beaches, vacationers will probably want to use the big public beaches elsewhere on the island. Public tennis is available in town and golf is nearby in West Chop. Evenings are quiet because the town does not have a liquor license, but there are many things to do: movies, theater, the lectures and courses sponsored throughout the year by the Nathan Mayhew Seminars, and year-round entertainment at the Katherine Cornell Theatre. Some of the inn and motel prices are a bit more modest than most places in Edgartown.

The Down-Island town of Oak Bluffs first became popular as a Methodist camp meeting place in the mid-nineteenth century and soon after became a very large summer resort, which it still is. It no longer has huge hotels (nearly all of them were destroyed by fire), but the summer frivolity and seaside boardwalk atmosphere prevail, along with its extraordinary Carpenter Gothic architecture. A merry-go-round, pizza and ice cream parlors, saltwater taffy stands, and shops cater to the tourists from the excursion boats running back and forth

to the Cape Cod towns of Falmouth and Hyannis. The town's U-shaped harbor is jammed with power boats, and there's a very attractive sandy beach that runs along either side of the ferry dock. There are public tennis courts and a golf course. The rates for rooms in Oak Bluffs are less than those at other places on the island.

The visual character of Edgartown evolved from whaling industry money made during the nineteenth century. With its handsome architecture, brick sidewalks, fences ablaze with roses, and beautiful gardens, it is the prettiest town on the island. Flags fly everywhere in Edgartown, another reminder of its maritime background. The majority of the Vineyard's hotels and inns are clustered in the village proper, where there's an endless array of restaurants, gift shops, boutiques, boat rentals, sailboat charters, the island's performing arts center, and one beach, all within walking distance. There are public tennis courts and two large public beaches within 3 miles of the center of town, and another beach and wildlife reservation on Chappaquiddick Island, a distance of 3 miles from the island's ferry. The town has become very congested in the summertime, so free parking lots outside of town and a shuttle bus service have been introduced.

To stay Up-Island, a car is a necessity, as it may be a 5- or 6-mile drive to a beach or a grocery store. With its many sparsely settled areas, it is very rural and quiet. West Tisbury, which cuts across the middle of the island from shore to shore, has very little beach access,

An Up-Island farm.

and the town's center seems more like a New England farming community than does any other place on the island. It has always been a farming community, the annual country fair is here, and there are several riding stables. Evening entertainment consists of old movies at the Agricultural Hall in the center of town, and there are lectures and musical programs at the Congregational Church. There are very few places to stay and most visitors rent private homes or beach cottages.

With its high, rolling hills and sweeping views of the Atlantic Ocean and Vineyard Sound, the Up-Island town of Chilmark is very beautiful. In recent years its land has become some of the most expensive on the island. Chilmark has no private clubs, but the community center is a gathering place for residents and visitors where there are sports—baseball, tennis, but no golf—lectures, concerts, nature walks, and programs for children. Chilmark center, called Beetlebung Corner, has a summer grocer, a very good restaurant, and a couple of shops, while Chilmark's fishing port of Menemsha has its own beach, several eating places, a couple of gift and clothing shops, a gas station, a grocer, a post office, and two fish markets. The picturesque harbor is small and crowded with fishing and pleasure boats. There are several places to stay in Chilmark; in addition, private homes can be rented.

The Indian town of Gay Head on the western tip of the island is a premier tourist attraction because of the Gay Head Cliffs. The cliffs have a restaurant, take-out food stands, and a cluster of tourist gift shops that cater to busloads of sightseers. There are few places to stay in the town other than private home rentals.

Wherever you decide to stay on the Vineyard, you'll find each town has its individual character emanating from its historic roots. The scope of things to do and the variety of places to go in each town have fascinated and delighted visitors since the nineteenth century.

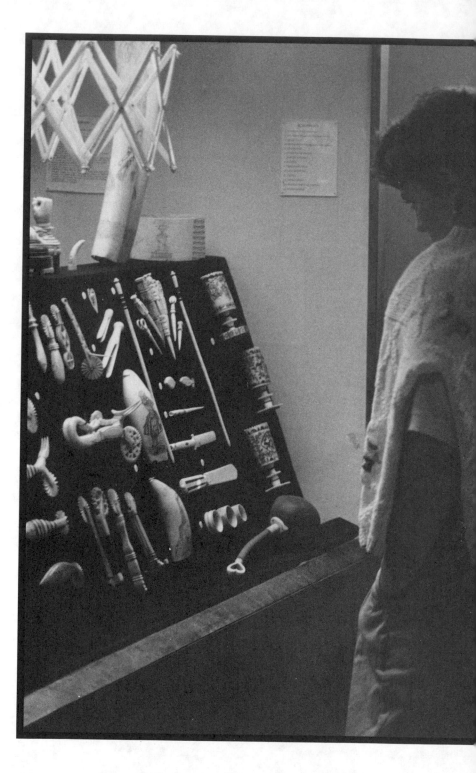

2

A BRIEF
HISTORY

There have been many theories and much speculation about early explorers landing on Nantucket, Martha's Vineyard, and Cape Cod, but the first written observations about the Vineyard were made by the Reverend John Brereton and Gabriel Archer, who sailed from England to these shores in 1602 aboard Captain Bartholomew Gosnold's ship. According to their reports and the authoritative research by two prominent English historians, David and Allison Quinn (published by the Hakluyt Society in London in 1983), they made their first landfall on Cape Pogue on Chappaquiddick. The Quinns noted, "the probability that it is Gosnold's first [sighting of] Martha's Vineyard is very high indeed."

They went ashore, and Brereton noted in his report: "Going around about it, we found it to be foure English miles in compasse without house or inhabitant. . . ." Both men were impressed by the vegetation and berries; the strawberries were "bigger than ours in England," and bushes—raspberries, blueberries, huckleberries, and grapevines—were familiar. Brereton continued, "Such an incredible store of vines, as well in the woodie part of the Island where they run vpon every tree, as on the outward parts, that we could not goe for treading vpon them." They were equally impressed with the ducks, geese, and other wildfowl, the beach peas growing on the sandy shore, and "huge bones and ribbes of whale." Archer wrote of similar impressions, but also stated, "we named it Martha's Vineyard," which historians believe was for Gosnold's daughter Martha and possibly for his mother-in-law, Martha Golding. The Vineyard part of the name came from the masses of grapevines they saw everywhere.

The vessel moved on to the main island, where they encountered American Indians (they had only seen evidence of inhabitants on Chappaquiddick). Brereton wrote: "Yet we found no townes, nor many of their houses, although we saw manie Indians, which are tall, big boned men, all naked, sauing they couer their priuy parts with a blacke tewed skin, much like a Black-smiths apron, tied about their middle and betweene their legs behinde: they gaue vs their fish readie boiled, (which they carried in a basket made of twigges). . . ." and shared their tobacco, which they smoked in pipes made of hard, dry clay. The Indian name for the island was Noepe, meaning "amid the waters."

These Indians were of the Pokanocket Confederacy, who inhabited the surrounding islands as well. Also called Wampanoags, meaning "Easterners," they belonged to the Algonquian linguistic group, which extended in a great semicircle from the Carolinas up into Canada and west to the Rocky Mountains. At the time the Pilgrims landed, Massasoit was the sachem, or chief, of the Algonquian confederation.

Gosnold weighed anchor and sailed up Vineyard Sound to Cutty-hunk Island, the outermost in the Elizabeth Island chain that stretches out from Woods Hole. They stayed most of the summer here and loaded their vessel with sassafras root, skins, and furs bartered from the friendly Indians before they returned to England.

It was forty years later, in 1641, that Thomas Mayhew of Watertown, Massachusetts, purchased for forty pounds the Vineyard, Nantucket, and the Elizabeth Islands from two English noblemen who held conflicting grants to the area. The following year his son, Thomas Mayhew, Jr., arrived with a group and chose Edgartown for the island's first white settlement. They called it Great Harbor. The town's official name was bestowed by Governor Lovelace of New York in 1671 (when Martha's Vineyard was for a time part of New York) in honor of Edgar, infant son of the duke of York, heir apparent to the British crown. Both Dutchess County and Queens County in New York were named at the same time. The town subsequently became the county seat for the Vineyard and the Elizabeth Islands.

These first settlers found the Indians to be a handsome, disciplined, and peaceful tribe, as Brereton had noted. The Indians' economy was

Whaling was Edgartown's principal industry in the nineteenth century. (top)

The paddle-wheel steamer Martha's Vineyard *leaves Oak Bluffs while vacationers wave from their catboats. (bottom)* (PHOTOGRAPHS COURTESY OF THE VINEYARD MUSEUM)

based on fishing and farming, rather than hunting, and they willingly shared their knowledge of taming the wilderness, whaling alongshore, gathering fruit and shellfish, seining the creeks for herring in the spring, catching cod and eel in the winter, hunting wild game, and

Looking "over Jordan" to the hotel and Camp Grounds in Oak Bluffs.
(COURTESY OF THE VINEYARD MUSEUM)

planting corn in the spring. Thomas Mayhew began his work to Christianize the friendly Indians, and the little settlement grew very slowly. (There were about eighty-five white people on the island in 1660.) Fifteen years later his son was the first of many islanders to perish at sea. Thomas Mayhew, Jr., had left Boston on a mission to England and his vessel was never heard from again.

His father continued to Christianize the Indians, as did three succeeding generations, earning themselves the name "Missionary Mayhews." They exercised an important influence over the island's growth and character. There was never open hostility between these settlers and the natives, although Governor Mayhew's authority as chief magistrate was eventually challenged by other settlers who accused the Mayhews of running a feudal state. As time passed, natives were edged off the richer lands on the island; the white settlers did, however, purchase these lands, not confiscate them. Some Indians moved off the island to the mainland, and others moved to Chappaquiddick or to Gay Head, which is now one of the two Indian townships in the state.

By tradition, these early English settlers were farmers, and gradually settlements other than Edgartown took root on the island. They became almost totally self-sufficient fishing and farming communities where boats and fishing gear were used equally with plows, wagons, and harrows. Not only were pigs, chickens, and cows in the barnyard, but great flocks of sheep roamed the moors. There were mills along the north shore to grind corn and make brick and paint from clay. Vineyarders wove their own cloth from the sheep's wool, evaporated the sea water for salt, hunted wild game, grew their own vegetables, and fashioned their farm tools on anvils.

From the earliest times, Vineyarders also looked to the sea and maritime trade for their livelihood. They exported cranberries, wool, candles, whale oil, and salt cod, which, with New England rum, were the basis of Yankee trade with the Catholic countries of Europe as well as the Azores, the Cape Verde Islands, and the West Indies. The growth of Vineyard Haven was directly proportionate to the expansion of maritime trade between the American colonies and the West Indies, as the town became a primary anchorage for vessels moving up and down the coast.

Whaling became Edgartown's principal industry. Although sheep farming on the island was successful, it was the sea, with its possibilities for adventure and profit, that lured man and boy down to the waterfront. For over two centuries the majority of Vineyard men earned their living as fishermen, merchant seamen, whalers, or pilots, sailing aboard barks, packets, coastwise schooners, sloops, and even clipper ships.

Edgartown and Vineyard Haven reached the peak of their prosperity

Fisherman's boat house in Menemsha decorated with swordfish tails.

in the nineteenth century. By 1914, the completion of the Cape Cod Canal and the increased movement of freight by steamship, train, and truck, rather than under sail, signaled the decline of Vineyard Haven's busy port. In addition, the discovery of petroleum in 1859 had undercut the whaling industry, whose end was hastened by the loss of Yankee ships during the Civil War; by World War I the industry was finished.

Changes came slowly, but they were irreversible. Oak Bluffs came into being as a popular Methodist camp meeting place in 1835, and eventually it became the island's first summer resort. The resort business became increasingly important through the years and has now replaced everything else and become the island's primary source of income. Despite all the changes, the towns have continued to retain their individual character: Edgartown with its handsome whaling captains' houses and stately elms; the summer holiday frivolity of Oak Bluffs' gingerbread architecture; Vineyard Haven, the island's commercial center; the farming community of West Tisbury, whose agricultural origins are still strong and seem far from the sea; the meeting of sea and soil in Chilmark, where grey, weathered farmhouses dot the rolling moors; Gay Head, still an Indian township; and Menemsha, which is the last true fishing village on the island.

Missouri muralist Thomas Hart Benton, a lifelong summer resident of Martha's Vineyard, rendered this painting of his Chilmark neighbor Josie West, a deaf mute farmer. Despite his handicaps, West supported himself by selling butter, eggs, milk, and mutton to summer visitors. An expert woodsman, he also sold firewood. (COURTESY OF THE VINEYARD MUSEUM)

3

WHEN
TO GO

Martha's Vineyard has four distinct seasons for the visitor to consider, and, of course, summer is the most popular season. The weather is very pleasant; with the prevailing southwest winds, the air temperature averages seventy degrees. On clear, brilliant days the sky is a radiant blue and the sea is a collage of vivid blues and greens. The island's many beaches are crowded with people tanning, playing in the sand, or swimming in the gentle Sound waters or the rolling surf along the south shore. The warm Gulf Stream offshore and the surrounding sandy shoals, which the sun warms more easily than deep water, cause the water temperature to range from the sixties to the low seventies.

At other times a smoky southwester blows all day, or a fog rolls in from offshore, misting the abundant, breathtaking roses and cloaking the harbors and beaches in muffled stillness. A mournful moan of a foghorn drones, and all boating traffic stays in port. On these days the towns are jammed as crowds flock in to shop, eat, or visit the museums and art galleries.

All summer long, there is a wide variety of entertainment nightly, and the typical summer resort activities are available during the day. There's also a constant flow of special events during July and August— house tours, auctions, art shows, parades, celebrations, festivals, fireworks, a sailing regatta, a road race, and a country fair.

This very busy holiday season comes to an abrupt end on Labor Day with an enormous exodus of visitors. Many people still come to the island through the early fall, but nowhere does it seem crowded. The wonderful weather lingers for weeks, because of the surrounding Sound and ocean that are slow to cool off. During those beautiful September and October days, when the water is still warm for hardy swimmers, a yellow haze hangs over the moors in the mornings, the middays are filled with a false warmth, and the evenings are cool. The still autumn nights are beautiful; the towns are quiet, and a harvest moon casts its glow across the still harbors, silhouetting the few ships riding at anchor.

Out on the beaches at this time of year, the beach plums have turned a succulent purple, the marsh grasses fringing the tidal ponds and the highbush blueberry turn a palette of fall colors, and purple asters and goldenrod blanket the fields Up-Island. The Beetlebung trees turn a brilliant red at Beetlebung Corner. The seaweed also has shed its summer growth. The shallow waters are crystal clear, and the slanting sun sparkles on the water like crumpled tinfoil. The ponds are filled with migrating birds. Summer residents are closing up their houses and cottages all through the fall. Shipyard workers are hauling and storing boats everywhere. Scallopers are busy launching their small workboats before October, when they start dragging for the succulent bivalve that is such an important part of the winter economy.

For the visitor at this halcyon time of year most of the shops and restaurants are open, although some have limited hours. One big fall attraction is the Fishing Derby from mid-September to mid-October. Tivoli Day in Oak Bluffs includes bicycle races and a street fair as well as several handcraft fairs. Aside from these two major scheduled events, there are many things for the visitor to do. There are nature walks, bird walks, sports from golf and tennis to horseback riding on the beach, movies, and occasional lectures and concerts. Picnicking on the beach at this time of year, tucked behind a dune if the wind comes up, can be delightful.

By late fall fewer restaurants and shops are open, but those that are gear up for the popular Thanksgiving Weekend. The inns are full, ferries are sold out on certain dates, private homes are reopened, and shops are brimming with Christmas gifts for visitors.

By now the Up-Island towns are very sparsely populated while the Down-Island towns, which relate much more closely to the mainland, begin to prepare for the Christmas holiday. All through the fall, many residents, young and old, have been working at various handcrafts and making jams and jellies in preparation for the Christmas season. By mid-December the handsome, white whaling captains' houses and beautiful churches are decorated with the traditional holly and greens. Edgartown's Main Street is lined with small Christmas trees running down to the waterfront where the fishing fleet comes in from offshore for the holiday. The second weekend in December, Edgartown has a special Christmas celebration, and many of the inns offer reduced rates for the weekend. For the visitor there are walking tours of the historic houses, holiday shopping, carols ringing out from the St. Andrews Church belfry, horse-drawn carriage rides around town, Christmas concerts at the Old Whaling Church, and a parade.

Winter on the Vineyard is very quiet and the weather is usually moderate, with an average temperature of thirty degrees. Snow lasts only a few days, but the dampness can be penetrating. Bone-chilling raw winds sweep across the empty beaches, and northeasters—sometimes as severe as a hurricane—batter the island and delay the ferries. Occasionally the harbors freeze over.

Even so, the winter population has increased in recent years. Both retired people and young men and women do handcrafts, art, carpentry, boatbuilding, and other occupations through this quiet season. There are winter activities for these residents and any visitors: a mid-

Summertime visitors and residents love the Vineyard's beaches. (left)

In the fall, the scallopers are busy launching their small workboats. (lower left)

Occasionally a severe storm batters the island. (bottom)

A major snowstorm is unusual on the Vineyard.

island ice-skating rink, two health spas, an amateur theater group, special programs at the performing arts center and the Katherine Cornell Theatre, and a large selection of lectures and courses at the Nathan Mayhew Seminars. Cross-country skiing on the beach and dunes is a special treat for as long as the snow lasts.

The ocean is slow to warm up, so spring comes slowly to the island; but as the days get longer and warmer, the pace begins to quicken. The cool, crisp May days, when the sky seems a particularly brilliant blue and white gulls soar overhead, are truly beautiful. The banging of hammers, the smell of paint—those white houses have to be painted all the time due to the salt air—the launching of boats, and the repairing of lobster pots by fishers in Menemsha are certain harbingers of another season approaching. Shops and restaurants once again clean, paint, and decorate to prepare for summer, which officially begins mid-June. Actually, most places open Memorial Day weekend or a bit earlier. As the days go by, houses and cottages are opened and gardens planted.

The shipyards accelerate their work schedules to a frenzied pace as they rush to paint, repair, and launch boats, and ferry reservations become harder to obtain without advance planning.

The visitor at this time of year will find the days crisp and cool, so swimming is out, but a picnic on the beach out of the cool wind coming off the water can be very pleasant. An early spring drive around the island is a joy, as the shadbush is in bloom—one of the first signs of spring—and its showery, white flowers cascade from its branches. The chirp of pinkletinks (the local name for spring peepers) can be heard from the ponds; along the roadways and sandy shores, white beach-plum blossoms burst into bloom. With the trees still bare and the beaches still empty, the island's outlines stand out vividly at this time of year, particularly when you view them from the Up-Island hills. From there, it looks as though the island has withdrawn a little while longer before being temporarily "loaned out" to visitors for another season.

Whatever the season you choose to come, you'll find this island unique and interesting.

During the spring, people keep busy sprucing up the island's houses and buildings for the summer tourist season.

4

HOW TO
GET THERE

You can reach Martha's Vineyard by air, by ferry, or in your own boat. Choosing which form of transportation to take will require some planning; your choice will be determined by how much time you have to spend in getting to the island and whether you will want your own car on the island. Even so, there are still many varied possibilities for travel to the island, such as do you drive to New Bedford and fly or ferry (without your car), or do you bus to Falmouth and ferry to the island?

Car

The most commonly used transportation to the island are the ferries and cruise boats, which sail from four different towns and are easily reached by car. One ferry port is New Bedford, an hour's drive south of Cape Cod on the Massachusetts coast. Two others are Woods Hole,

Everyone's favorite old workhorse, the ferry Islander *operates year-round between Woods Hole and Vineyard Haven. Backgammon and card games are popular with some passengers who commute daily to and from the mainland.*

which is at the beginning, or shoulder, of Cape Cod, and Falmouth, adjacent to Woods Hole. Ferries also originate in Hyannis, which is midway along the south shore of the Cape (locally referred to as the mid-Cape area).

To get to the Cape, it might be helpful for you to know the mileage from key cities.

Washington, D. C.—Woods Hole .... 478 miles
New York—Woods Hole .... 245 miles
Hartford, Conn.—Woods Hole .... 140 miles
Providence, R. I.—Woods Hole .... 77 miles
Boston—Woods Hole .... 85 miles

It is about 20 miles from the Cape Cod Canal to Hyannis or Falmouth and a bit longer to Woods Hole.

With the summer traffic, it can take you longer to reach the Cape than at other times of the year, so be sure to allow yourself extra driving time. It might take an hour to drive from the Cape Cod Canal to Hyannis in summer traffic.

Driving from New York City to Woods Hole may take six hours. Take I-95 to Providence; from there, take I-195 east to Cape Cod. There are numerous signs to the Cape and Islands. At the Bourne Bridge, which spans the Cape Cod Canal, follow the signs to Falmouth and Woods Hole. As you enter Falmouth, you'll see a large Steamship Authority parking lot for those who want to leave their cars on the mainland. There is a shuttle bus service from this parking lot down to the ferry at Woods Hole.

From Boston to Woods Hole is about a two-hour drive in moderate traffic, but it can be much longer in heavy summer traffic. From downtown Boston take the Southeast Expressway (Route 3), turn right just before the Sagamore Bridge (which also spans the Cape Cod Canal), follow the canal for 3 miles to the Bourne Bridge, and follow the signs to Falmouth. If you're going to Hyannis, take the Sagamore Bridge over the Cape Cod Canal, and continue on the mid-Cape highway (Route 6) to Route 132, which leads down to Hyannis.

If you're planning to leave your car on the mainland, you'll save an hour or more in driving time by taking the New Bedford ferry, which is for passengers only. Take Exit 15 in New Bedford and head south toward the waterfront. Follow the Vineyard Ferry signs to Leonard's Wharf. The parking lot is a distance from the ferry wharf, so allow yourself plenty of time.

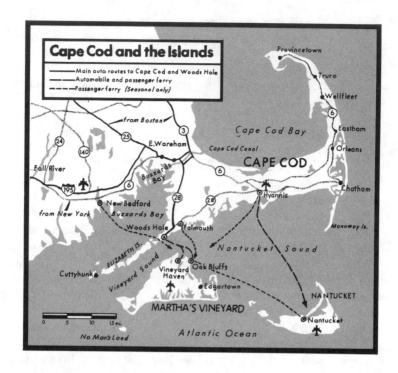

Cape Cod and the Islands

──────── Main auto routes to Cape Cod and Woods Hole
──────── Automobile and passenger ferry
- - - - - - Passenger ferry (Seasonal only)

Provincetown

Truro

Wellfleet

from Boston

Cape Cod Bay

Eastham

E.Wareham

Cape Cod Canal

Orleans

CAPE COD

Fall River

Buzzards Bay

Chatham

New Bedford

Hyannis

from New York

Buzzards Bay

Woods Hole

Falmouth

Monomoy Is.

ELIZABETH IS.

Nantucket Sound

Cuttyhunk

Vineyard Sound

Oak Bluffs

Vineyard Haven

Edgartown

NANTUCKET

MARTHA'S VINEYARD

0   5   10   15 mi.

Nantucket

No Man's Land

Atlantic Ocean

A regular summer activity among children is diving for coins alongside the Oak Bluffs ferry wharf. (right)

Many people come to the Vineyard in their own boats. (below)

Train and Bus

There is Amtrak rail service from New York City and points south to Providence and Boston, where bus service is available to Hyannis and Woods Hole. Bonanza Bus Lines provides frequent bus service between Boston and Woods Hole or Boston and Hyannis.

Bus service is also provided to Hyannis and Woods Hole from the New York City Port Authority Terminal (212–564–8484). Bonanza meets all Woods Hole ferries, providing direct service to the center of Boston (Greyhound Bus Terminal 617–423–5810) and Logan Airport. There is also a private limousine service from the Woods Hole ferry dock to Boston, Logan Airport, or other cities you request.

Cruise Ship and Ferry

If you leave your car on the mainland when you visit the Vineyard, you have more choices as to which cruise ship to take. There are three places where these ships originate: in New Bedford, which avoids all the Cape Cod congestion and summer traffic; in Woods Hole or Falmouth at the beginning of the Cape (or what is locally known as the

Feeding the seagulls that follow the ferries back and forth all summer long.

upper Cape); or in Hyannis, which is midway along the south shore of the Cape. Hyannis may be a good choice if you are staying on the Cape and visiting the Vineyard.

The New Bedford ferry lands in Vineyard Haven, the Falmouth and Hyannis ferries go to Oak Bluffs, and the Woods Hole ferry (the only one to take cars) runs to Vineyard Haven and Oak Bluffs.

The New Bedford, Martha's Vineyard cruise ship *Schamonchi,* which carries passengers and bicycles only, sails daily from Leonard's Wharf. The cruise across Buzzards Bay and down Vineyard Sound to Vineyard Haven is one hour and forty-five minutes. The ship has a cocktail and snack bar and makes three trips a day and four on weekends. It operates spring through fall, and no reservations are needed. The one-way fare is $8.50 for adults and $4.50 for children ages 5 through 12; for those under 5, it's free. A bicycle costs $2. Call (508) 997–1688 for more information.

From Falmouth Harbor, the *Island Queen,* a small, very pleasant cruise ship, sails to Oak Bluffs eight times a day from mid-June to mid-September. Four trips are made from mid-September to mid-October on weekdays. Late boats run on weekends only. The *Island Queen* carries passengers and bicycles only, and snack food is sold on the ship. It is a forty-minute ride. Adult fare one way is $5, or $9 round-trip. Children under 13 are $2.50 one way and $4 round-trip. Bicycles are $3 one way and $6 round-trip. Call (508) 548–4800 for more information. The company also has special buses that meet the morning trips for a complete, two-and-one-half-hour narrated tour of the island.

Hy-line Cruises operates boats from the Ocean Street dock in Hyannis to Oak Bluffs, making several trips a day from late April through October. They carry passengers and bicycles only, and have a snack bar and cocktail lounge. It takes one and a half hours to cruise across the Sound to the island. Adult fare one way is $10.50. The one-way fare for kids ages 5 through 12 is $5.25, and children 4 and under ride free. Bicycles are $4.50 one way. Hy-line also runs a ferry from Oak Bluffs to Nantucket. Adults pay $10.50 one way, children 12 and under are $5.25. Call (508) 693-0112 or (508) 778–2600 for more information.

The Woods Hole, Martha's Vineyard and Nantucket Steamship Authority is the only ferry line to the Vineyard that carries cars as well as bicycles and passengers. It also carries the greatest number of passengers. It has as many as fifteen boats a day from Woods Hole to Vineyard Haven or Oak Bluffs. It is a forty-five minute trip to either town. Car reservations must be made weeks in advance for the busy season. For information and advance automobile reservations, call (508) 540–2022. The telephones get very busy, so if you are on the island, the best thing to do is to go to the reservation office at the Martha's Vineyard Airport. The Authority's mailing address is P.O. Box 284, Woods Hole, Massachusetts, 02543. In season, the one-way charge is $36 for car and driver. From mid-October through November the charge is $23 and from December to mid-March $17. Bicycle fare one way is $2.75. Adult fare, one way, is $4.50 and children ages 5 to 12 pay half fare. All the Authority's boats have snack bars.

Bear in mind that all ferries are subject to small price increases from time to time. If you plan to leave your car on the mainland, you may park in the lot owned by the ferry company. They average about $7 per day. If you do bring your car, be sure to be there thirty minutes before sailing time.

There are now new penalties for changing or canceling auto reservations. Be sure to check with the Authority.

Private Boat

If you'd like to sail to the island in your own boat, there are four harbors offering dockage facilities. Menemsha, at the western end of the island, has a small, attractive harbor with slips that provide electricity. For details call the harbormaster at (508) 645–2846. Vineyard Haven has moorings, dockage with plug-ins, launch service, and marina services. The harbormaster can be reached at (508) 693–4200. Oak Bluffs has a tightly packed, U-shaped harbor. Motorboat or sailboat slips with plug-ins and marina services are available, and there are some moorings out in the harbor. The harbormaster is at (508) 693–4355. Edgartown has no plug-in facilities, which has helped to keep the waterfront from becoming too cluttered. Moorings out in the harbor are available for rent by the day, week, or season. The shipyard provides marina services. For details call the harbormaster at (508) 627–4746.

There are now two pump-out facilities for boats in Edgartown harbor: the town dock and a barge from the shipyard. After extensive studies, Edgartown has initiated innovative regulations to keep the harbor clean, and they are strictly enforced.

Plane

Air traffic in and out of Martha's Vineyard has increased dramatically in recent years. The airline carriers serving the island constantly vary, but there is always year-round service from the New York area (currently

Newark, New Jersey), Boston, New Bedford, Hyannis, and Nantucket. There also may be seasonal service from Westchester County in New York and Bridgeport or Hartford in Connecticut. It is best to check with your travel agent or the Martha's Vineyard Chamber of Commerce to find out which airlines are currently operating.

Check with your travel agent for air fare from the New York City area. From Boston it is $90 one way. From New Bedford, Hyannis, and Nantucket it is $34 one way, without advance reservations.

Taxis meet all regularly scheduled flights at the Martha's Vineyard Airport, and there are several car rental dealers at the airport.

Private planes have access to the Martha's Vineyard Airport, but in the height of the summer season there may be so much congestion that you should call ahead to make sure there is adequate space for your plane. Call (508) 693-4776. Private planes also land at the small airport in Edgartown, where the landing field is a grass strip.

5

HOW TO GET AROUND

I f you arrive on the Vineyard without your own form of transportation, you will be pleased to find taxis and buses available, as well as car, bicycle, and moped rentals.

Taxi

Taxis meet all the ferries and scheduled plane flights. Taxi fare between any of the Down-Island towns and the Martha's Vineyard Airport is $10. West of the airport, to the towns of West Tisbury, Chilmark, Menemsha, and Gay Head, the general charge is $30 to $35 per hour for up to four passengers.

Some year-round taxi companies serving the Down-Island towns are:
Marlene's Taxi, Vineyard Haven, 693–0037.
Adam Cab, Edgartown, 627–4462.
Upisland Taxi, Oak Bluffs, 627–4566 or 693–5454.
Atlantic Cab, Oak Bluffs, 693–7110.
All Island Taxi, Vineyard Haven, 693–3705 or 1–800–540–3705.

Bus

There is shuttle bus service between the three Down-Island towns from mid-May to mid-October. In the summer season the buses run twice an hour, and during the spring and fall they run hourly. The bus stops in the three towns are next to the ferry ticket office in Vineyard Haven, behind the police station beside Ocean Park in Oak Bluffs, and on Church Street across from the Old Whaling Church in Edgartown.

Edgartown provides a seasonal bus service from the outside of town into the center of town. You may park your car on the edge of Edgartown in the parking lot behind the Edgartown General Stores, where the Beach Road and the inland road to Vineyard Haven converge. You also may park in the school parking lot just off upper Main Street. Parking is free. The buses run every fifteen minutes to downtown. It is advisable to use this bus system as parking in Edgartown and traffic congestion become big problems in the summertime. The other Edgartown shuttle service, the open Tivoli Trolley Bus, leaves from Church and Main streets by the Whaling Church and goes to South Beach every half hour. The ride costs $1.50.

There also are tour buses in Vineyard Haven and Oak Bluffs that meet the ferries and offer around-the-island tours. Advance reservations are not necessary. The trip around the island takes about two hours, and those buses that go out to Gay Head Cliffs stay long enough for the passengers to get a quick lunch at one of the food take-out places there. Taxi vans also meet the ferries at Vineyard Haven. Passengers can share the van, if they wish, for a sightseeing tour. The charge is $30 and up, depending on the number of passengers and the length of time for the tour.

Bicycle, Moped, and Car Rental

These rentals are available in the three Down-Island towns. The majority are in Vineyard Haven, clustered near the ferry dock, while those in Oak Bluffs are, for the most part, right at the beginning of Circuit Avenue and the adjacent harbor area. Edgartown has the fewest rental places, and no moped rentals.

Listings of all types of vehicles can be found in both the yellow pages of the local phone book and the newspapers. The car rentals include Hertz, National, Colonial, and Atlantic.

To rent a car during the busiest times in mid-summer or on big holiday weekends, it's best to reserve one ahead of time. Ask the hotel or inn for assistance, or check with your local travel agent.

Bicycling

Bicycling on the island is a great deal of fun because the Vineyard has varied terrain. It will be helpful for you to know the distances and terrain if you're thinking about bicycling around the island. Look for the bike paths in many areas.

From Vineyard Haven to:
Oak Bluffs (via shore route), *flat, one hill* .... 3.4 miles
Edgartown (via shore route), *flat, one hill* .... 7 miles
Edgartown (on the inland road), *hilly* ....7 miles
West Tisbury, *partly hilly* ....7 miles
Chilmark Center, *hilly* ....12 miles
Gay Head, *very hilly* ....19 miles
Airport, *partly hilly* ....5 miles

From Oak Bluffs to:
Edgartown (via shore route), *flat* .... 5.5 miles
South Beach at Katama, *flat* .... 9 miles
Gay Head, *hilly* .... 20 miles
Chilmark (via Airport Road), *partly hilly* .... 16 miles

Bicycles are a popular means of transportation on the island.

From Edgartown to:

South Beach at Katama, *flat*	3 miles
West Tisbury, *hilly*	8.5 miles
Airport, *hilly*	4.5 miles
Cape Pogue and Wasque Wildlife Sanctuaries on Chappy	3 miles

From West Tisbury to:

Chilmark Center, *hilly*	5.4 miles
Gay Head, *very hilly*	10.5 miles

From Chilmark Center to:

Gay Head, *very hilly*	6 miles
Menemsha, *one hill*	2 miles
Menemsha to North Tisbury (via the North Road), *hilly*	6.5 miles

From North Tisbury to:

Vineyard Haven (via the State Road), *one hill*	6.5 miles
The Lambert's Cove Road, a loop off State Road, *hilly*	4.5 miles

There are special bike paths between Oak Bluffs and Edgartown, between Vineyard Haven and Edgartown on the inland road, and alongside the state forest on the Edgartown–West Tisbury Road. More are being planned, so watch for them.

Locking up your bicycle while you do errands or go sightseeing in the three Down-Island towns is necessary because of the enormous number of bike riders on the island. The towns now have bike racks as follows:

Vineyard Haven: on Main Street straight up from the ferry; beside the ferry wharf; two blocks to your right after you come up Union Street from the ferry wharf; and out on the beach road toward Oak Bluffs at the Information Center.

Oak Bluffs: at the beginning of Circuit Avenue across from the merry-go-round; by the public rest rooms next to the ferry ticket office; and behind the police station next to the town hall. No bikes or mopeds are allowed on the main street, Circuit Avenue.

Edgartown: in the town parking lot at the foot of Main Street; on Pease Point Way, a half-block to your left off upper Main Street; and at the town dock beside the Chappaquiddick Ferry office. No bikes or mopeds are allowed in the center of Edgartown.

6

WHERE
TO STAY

Your choice of a place to stay on the Vineyard will depend on the type of holiday you prefer. Every sort of lodging is available, including inns, hotels, motels, rental houses, efficiency apartments, cottages, campgrounds, and a hostel (though you will not find all of these in every town). A complete list of accommodations is available from the Chamber of Commerce; the following list consists of the author's recommendations.

With few exceptions, the inns on the island resemble bed and breakfast places in other areas. Some are very elegant, while others are simple. Most provide a continental breakfast, and some serve a full breakfast. A few places with dining rooms that are open for lunch and dinner also serve the general public.

Most of the historic inns are furnished with antiques and have limited outdoor space, so they are not appropriate for small children. The efficiency apartments or larger hotels with separate cottages that have open grounds and a pool or beach are much more relaxing for a family.

Some places are open on a seasonal basis, from early spring to the middle of autumn. Most places are open year-round. The rates vary according to the seasons. The general rule of thumb is that summer (in season) is from June to mid-September. Spring and fall rates encompass April, May, and mid-September to mid-November. Winter rates at year-round places are the least costly. In-season prices can range from $70 per night for a double room to $300 and up for a two-bedroom suite in the finest places.

If you're planning a week's stay, apartments, cottages, or two-room suites with kitchenettes are convenient and economical. Prices for these efficiency units range from $350 to $1,500 per week, depending on location, size, and number of occupants. Off-season rates are at least 30 percent less; it's best to inquire about them.

Private homes are available through various real estate offices in the towns. Most are listed with the chamber of commerce. Rates run from a few thousand dollars per month to over $30,000 for the largest waterfront homes. On-site inspection is always the best idea for any long-term rentals.

If you are planning a summer visit to the island, the earlier you make your reservation the better; January is not too soon. If you wait until spring you may not be able to obtain your first choice in the hotels or inns, some of which have cottages and suites that are always in demand.

In this guide, the general in-season price range per night is as follows: expensive, $150 and up; moderate, $100–$150; inexpensive, $50–$100. Most places are in the moderate range.

EDGARTOWN

There are many inns, hotels, shops, and restaurants within easy walking distance in this town, and three large public beaches within 2 or 3 miles of town. Edgartown is especially popular in the summer months, so be sure to make a reservation as early as possible. The following is a selection of some of the charming places to stay.

Inns

Point Way Inn
Main Street
(508) 627–8633
Open year-round. Bed and breakfast. Moderate to expensive.

In the garden of this 150-year-old whaling captain's house are a lush, green professional croquet court and a charming, ivy-covered gazebo where tea and lemonade are served in the afternoon.

Ben Smith, the owner, who left a law practice and went to sea, bought the inn one day when he and his wife had put in to Edgartown in a storm. They have redecorated it with character and individuality. There is a handsome library flanking the fireplace wall, a wet bar, nautical mementos of Ben's maritime heritage, a sunny breakfast room warmed by a Franklin stove, and lovely antiques in the bedrooms

The Charlotte Inn
South Summer Street
(508) 627–4751
Open year-round. Moderate to expensive.

There are several nineteenth-century houses in this inn complex, which has beautifully landscaped grounds. The rooms are furnished with French and English antiques. A complimentary continental breakfast is included, and a full breakfast is available. The inn's restaurant, L'etoile, serves lunch and dinner to the general public and has limited hours in the winter.

The Point Way Inn in Edgartown has a professional croquet court, and after-noon tea is served in this charming gazebo.

The Daggett Houses
North Water Street
(508) 627–4600
Open year-round. Bed and breakfast. Moderate to expensive.

The original part of this historic building, the breakfast room, is on the lower level and opens onto a lawn that stretches down to the waterfront. The owners call it the Chimney Room, due to the unique beehive construction of the fireplace, said to be similar to one built in Plymouth, Massachusetts, in 1667. Originally the room was the first tavern on Martha's Vineyard to sell beer and ale. In 1660 the "taverner," John Daggett, was fined five shillings for "selling strong liquor." In 1750 the Daggett House was added onto the tavern; it is the only foursquare hip-roof house in the village. Through the years the Daggett House has been used for a customs house, a sailor's boarding-house, a store, and during the whaling era, a counting house.

Outside the tavern room, on the lawn, is the garden cottage, which has three double rooms with baths. The building was once a private school, and on the wall there's a framed receipt, dated 1857 and signed by Catherine Bassett, acknowledging payment of $1.68 from Captain Theodore Wimpenny for twelve weeks of instruction for Master Theodore.

Across North Water Street another house has been added to the inn. Called the Warren House, it consists of efficiency units. The main house has regular bedrooms plus two suites facing the harbor, and all rooms now have telephones. There is no quaint pretense here, and the cellar dining room looks more like our image of an eighteenth-century tavern than does any other place on the island. Centuries old pine paneling and beams, a brass flintlock blunderbuss, whale harpoons, primitive iron Betty lamps and old whale oil lamps decorate the room. Behind the handsome fireplace is a secret staircase, probably installed during the China Trade era when the house was a customs house (to avoid taxes). It never fails to fascinate and delight visitors. The room opens onto a long sweep of lawn down to the waterfront, and guests are served a delicious complimentary breakfast daily and the wonderful, limited-menu, moderately priced dinners by reservation only Thursday through Saturday. The restaurant is open to the public. Beer and wine are available.

The Shiverick Inn
Pease Point Way
(508) 627–3797
Open year-round. Bed and breakfast. Expensive.

Built in 1840 during the height of the whaling era by the town's leading physician, this is one of Edgartown's most elegant inns. Although it was originally a foursquare Greek Revival house, additions and changes were made through the years, many by the original owner's widow, who was impressed by the grandeur of southern mansions. The large front hall with high ceilings, sweeping staircase, and early maritime paintings is a striking introduction to the taste with which the rooms have been decorated. Through the front hall is a bright, cheerful sun room, an adjoining breakfast room, and a small terrace. On the second floor there are eleven large rooms with baths and an outside deck for all the guests to use as well as a two-room suite. The attractive rooms are furnished with antiques and decorated with pretty country wallpapers, and they have a great deal of charm. A light, regular breakfast is included, and they have bicycles to rent.

The Edgartown Inn
North Water Street
(508) 627–4794
Seasonal. Bed and breakfast. Moderate to expensive.

Profits from a successful whaling voyage around the Horn to the Pacific in 1798 enabled Captain Thomas Worth to build this home. His son, William Jenkins Worth, was successful in a different type of career when he became a hero in the Mexican-American War and gave Fort Worth, Texas, its name. The second owner turned the house into an inn, and it has been one ever since.

Through the years, well-known historical figures have stayed at the inn, including Daniel Webster. He was denied admittance at first, because his dark skin made him appear to be an American Indian, but later on he returned as a guest. Nathaniel Hawthorne came for a rest, and he not only became romantically linked with the innkeeper's daughter, but was inspired to write *Twice Told Tales* during his stay.

Located close to the center of the village, the inn is decorated with Victorian and other antiques, and there are interesting artifacts everywhere. The door of each of the twelve rooms in the main house has a brass plaque with the name of someone who was part of the inn's long history. A delicious country breakfast is served in the attractive, open courtyard in back as well as in the colorful breakfast room.

Across the courtyard, the Garden House has two spacious rooms with balconies, each room furnished with white wicker and decorated with delightful, summery Laura Ashley type curtains, wallpapers, and bedding. Adjacent to the Garden House is The Barn, which also has flowery decorating in rooms that have either private or semiprivate baths.

In the fall and spring, the inn offers midweek specials that are exceptionally inexpensive and a real find for such a charming hostelry.

The Colonial Inn
North Water Street
(508) 726–4711
Open year-round. Moderate to expensive.

"No effort will be spared to promote the comfort and pleasure of all guests," the *Vineyard Gazzette* reported in 1911 when this large building in Edgartown's center was complete. Remodeled several times in the intervening years, the first floor is now a complex of shops, and the second, third, and fourth floors are guest rooms and suites.

The forty-two rooms are light and airy and of ample size. They are simply decorated with brass beds, a natural wood armoire for the color cable television, private baths, air conditioning, and telephone. On the fourth floor, a small porch provides a spectacular view of Edgartown Harbor out to South Beach and over Chappaquiddick Island. The inn serves a continental breakfast, and a full breakfast is available in several restaurants nearby.

The Shiretown Inn
North Water Street
(508) 627–3353
Seasonal. Bed and breakfast. Inexpensive to moderate.

The two adjoining eighteenth-century houses that make up the inn have the small, original rooms typical of this early period and other rooms that have been opened up to provide a suite. They are decorated mostly in furniture of the late Victorian period, and all have private baths. Some have their own private entrances.

Behind the small, intimate courtyard in the back is a most attractive dining room in a separate building. A complimentary breakfast is served here for guests, and dinner is available to the general public. Behind the dining area is a row of old carriage houses that have been converted into inexpensive small, plain motel rooms. There is off-street parking.

Hotels

Harborside Inn
South Water Street
(508) 627–4321
Seasonal. Handicapped access on ground floor. Moderate to expensive.

A step off Main Street are three large whaling captains' houses with the names of the original owners over the doorways. Inside, and beyond, the buildings have been radically changed and enlarged. With two newer buildings on either side, the Harborside Inn now is a U-shaped, large resort complex around a swimming pool and boat piers that extend out into the harbor. There are both motorboats and sailboats for rent here, and sailing instruction also is available. Adjacent to the complex is the Navigator Restaurant and Boat Bar. Many rooms have balconies looking out on the harbor. No meals are included in the room cost.

The Edgartown Heritage Hotel
Upper Main Street
(508) 627–5161
Open year-round. Handicapped access. Inexpensive to moderate.

This contemporary, thirty-four–room hotel is tastefully decorated in reproduction antiques. The rooms are cheerful and large with modern baths, color television (satellite system), radio, individual telephones, and air conditioning. They serve a continental breakfast, and next door the Beeftender Restaurant, which is open for dinner, is very good. There are conference rooms, and a hair salon is on the premises. The individually climate-controlled rooms make it very comfortable in the off-season. There is ample parking in the rear.

The Harborview Hotel
Starbuck Neck
(508) 627–7000
Open year-round. Handicapped access. Expensive.

This grande dame of Vineyard hotels, whose original 1891 building is now restored, is a beloved island landmark. The 127 bright, cheery rooms, including the modern addition in the rear, have private baths, telephones, air conditioning, and color television. The apartments and white clapboard townhouses in this twelve-acre complex have fully equipped kitchens, and they are ideal for children.

The front veranda of the original building is furnished with period-piece old-fashioned rocking chairs where guests may enjoy a sweeping view across the pond to the handsome Edgartown Lighthouse, which marks the entrance to Edgartown Harbor. Sailboats and yachts move through the outer harbor, and Chappaquiddick Island is in the distance. There are tennis courts, a large pool surrounded by lush gardens and a croquet court in the back, and the swimming beach by the lighthouse in the front. This gracious jewel has been an island favorite for over a century.

The hotel provides baby-sitting, laundry, and valet services. There's a very attractive cafe and a large, first-rate dining room serving breakfast, lunch, and dinner.

The Kelly House
Kelly Street
(508) 627–7900
Seasonal. Handicapped access. Expensive.

The main building was an eighteenth-century inn, but there are now several more buildings, which comprise sixty rooms in all. While the colonial decor is charming, such modern conveniences as a television, air conditioning, and a telephone in each room are welcome, and there's a complimentary continental breakfast. A swimming pool and the inn's tennis courts are nearby, and baby-sitting, valet, and laundry services are provided. Located in the center of town, it's adjacent to, but not on, the harbor. The inn's pub, with the original eighteenth-century rough-hewn beams and ballast brick walls, is delightful, as is the light fare served from 11:00 A.M. to 11:00 P.M. daily.

Apartments

Chirgwin Apartments
North Summer Street
(508) 627–4745
Seasonal. Inexpensive.

Trim and neat, economical and very quiet, but only two blocks from the center of town, these four cottage units are a real find in Edgartown. They are available by the week. Bright and cheery, they have contemporary motel furnishings and telephones.

Edgartown Commons
Pease Point Way
(508) 627–4671
Seasonal. Inexpensive.

Two blocks from the center of town is a complex of thirty-five efficiency apartments with motel rooms and a playground area with swings, sandbox, and slides. There is a small, fenced-in pool and shuffleboard on the grounds. All the units have kitchens and color television. The largest of the units, simply furnished in a conventional manner, can accommodate six people; it has two bedrooms and a sofa bed in the living room. There is ample parking. Some apartments are in the large, old main building, which was originally the North School. The small lane running between the back of this building and the pool area is Mill Street, once the site of one of the town's gristmills.

Katama Shores Inn
South Beach
(508) 627–4747
Seasonal. Handicapped access on ground floor. Inexpensive.

Three miles from Edgartown on the Atlantic Ocean is the South Beach, which is called Katama (an Indian name meaning "great fishing place") by most people. It was here that a large Navy barracks was built during World War II. It has become, with remodeling and numerous additions, a hotel complex of sixty-seven units of rooms, suites, and cottages. All rooms have a private bath, television, telephone, and refrigerator, and some have kitchenettes. The largest cottage on the grounds has six rooms, a porch, a fireplace, and a grill; it is available by the week only.
Surrounded by open fields, it is just a five-minute walk over the dunes to the ocean beach. Ideal for children, it is plain but convenient, and accommodations include tennis, heated swimming pool, shuffleboard, bicycle rentals, and a restaurant open for breakfast, lunch, and dinner.

OAK BLUFFS

There are many bed and breakfast places in Oak Bluffs, but only one large, old-fashioned hotel and one attractive motel a half-mile from town. Many vacationers live on their powerboats or rent one of the little gingerbread-trimmed houses.

Island Inn
Beach Road (P.O. Box 1585)
(508) 693–2002
Open year-round. Handicapped access. Moderate to expensive.

This sprawling motel complex is set in a grove of oak and pine trees overlooking a golf course and Nantucket Sound. Each of the fifty-one units has a kitchen, fireplace, private bath, color television, telephone, and air conditioning, and they are much more tastefully decorated than the average motel room. One new, two-story building in the complex has high ceilings with bleached timbers and post-and-beam construction. Some rooms have a circular staircase to a loft bedroom with bath. The older suites are a bit larger than other rooms. The cabins facing the golf course have their own porches. Convenient for families with childern, the complex has tennis courts, a swimming pool, and a very good restaurant serving breakfast, lunch, and dinner.

The Oak House
Seaview and Pequot Avenue (P.O. Box 299)
(508) 693–4187
May–September. Bed and breakfast. Inexpensive.

A few blocks from the center of Oak Bluffs, on the shore road to Edgartown, is this large Victorian home, the summer residence of Massachusetts Governor Claflin in the 1870s. The house has dark-stained oak paneling everywhere and period-piece wicker and Victorian furniture. Guests can enjoy the sun room and the spacious living room with its piano. The handsome exterior has a large, open veranda enclosed by a magnificently carved railing and pastel-painted, fancy shingles. The ten guest rooms, four with shared baths, are bright and sunny. Many look out on Nantucket Sound, which is just across the road. A continental breakfast is served.

The Wesley Hotel
Lake Avenue (P.O. Box 1207)
(508) 693–6611
Seasonal. Bed and breakfast. Handicapped access. Moderate.

Near the center of town, facing Oak Bluffs Harbor, is this four-story, gingerbread-trimmed hotel remaining from the turn of the century when Oak Bluffs was in its heyday. At that time, there were several huge hotels in town, but they were eventually destroyed by fire.

The terrace of the Lothrop Merry House overlooking Vineyard Haven Harbor where a continental breakfast is served. Guests can also take a swim before breakfast. (right)

The Shiverick Inn, a bed and breakfast inn in Edgartown, is decorated for the Christmas holidays. (below)

For five generations the same family had owned and managed this island landmark. The hotel was completely renovated in the 1980s. The striking exterior with its rococo, Carpenter Gothic trim has a long veranda facing the busy Oak Bluffs Harbor, which is just across the street. The foyer has retained its antique decor, including an old-fashioned registration desk, heavy, dark-stained oak trim, and old photographs on the wall; an attractive cocktail lounge has been added. The first floor (formerly the dining room) has some new bedrooms that are especially convenient for the handicapped. Until the bedrooms were remodeled and redecorated in comfortable reproduction furnishings, there were old brass beds, claw-foot bathtubs, and basins in some of the bedrooms (amenities popular in Victorian hotels at the turn of the century). Continental breakfast is served.

The front rooms look out to the harbor filled with powerboats and the ferries that run back and forth to Cape Cod.

VINEYARD HAVEN

Vineyard Haven, the island's business center, has a few places to stay within easy walking distance of the town. It has many shops and some good restaurants, but because it is a dry town, it is much quieter in the evening than are Oak Bluffs and Edgartown. It has one small town beach near the ferry wharf, and boat, bike, car, moped, and sailboard rentals are easily available along the waterfront. The town has a large residential area heading out toward the West Chop Lighthouse, where there are many house rentals. You may bring your own alcoholic beverages.

Captain Dexter House
100 Main Street (P.O. Box 2457)
(508) 693–6564
Seasonal. Bed and breakfast. Moderate.

Captain Rodolphus Dexter's former home, built in 1843, is just as one imagines an exquisitely furnished mid-nineteenth-century home should look. The oriental rugs, early American oil paintings, antique brasses, Hepplewhite dining room table where a complimentary breakfast is served, and Rose Medallion porcelains are exceptional. The eight guest rooms, with beautiful quilts on the antique canopied beds and wallpapers and curtains in soft colors, are charming. Most rooms have private baths and some have fireplaces. The inn is only a block from the center of town, and there is ample parking. Bring your own alcoholic beverages.

The Thorncroft Inn
278 Main Street (P.O. Box 1022)
(508) 693–3333
Open year-round. Moderate to expensive.

In a delightfully quiet, woodland setting a mile from town, this rambling structure and several smaller buildings on the property are well known for their special appointments: large, tastefully decorated rooms with canopied beds; wood-burning fireplaces; central air conditioning; Jacuzzis or hot tubs in some rooms; TV on request; a full complimentary breakfast, and the *Boston Globe* at your door each morning.

Both afternoon tea and dinner are served to guests, and the inn is entirely nonsmoking. Bring your own alcoholic beverages. The inn is a well-deserved recipient of the AAA Four Diamond Award.

Lothrop Merry House
Owen Park
(508) 693–1646
Open year-round. Bed and breakfast. Inexpensive to moderate.

With a broad sweep of lawn reaching down to the beach, a continental breakfast served on the brick terrace overlooking the harbor, and

Launching a catboat in Vineyard Haven.

antique-filled rooms with fireplaces, this eighteenth-century guest house will fulfill the expectations of many visitors with its historic character.

There are seven rooms, four with private baths, and both a canoe and a Sunfish are available for guests. The owners also offer guests half-day, full-day, and overnight sails to the surrounding islands on their handsome, 54-foot Alden ketch. In the winter the owners head south to run a charter service in the Caribbean.

Ocean Side Inn
P.O. Box 2700
(508) 693–1296
Open May–November. Bed and breakfast. Handicapped access.
Moderate.

The view is spectacular from this newly converted home overlooking Vineyard Haven Harbor, only half a block from the center of town. Quiet and private, the inn has spacious grounds reaching down to a sandy beach. The bright, cheerful rooms have televisions, air conditioning, and private baths. There's a complimentary continental breakfast in the summer and ample parking space

WEST TISBURY

This farming community, which cuts across the middle of the island, is about a twenty-minute drive from the Down-Island towns. It has beaches for residents on the north and south shores and is a charming scenic area with several riding stables. It has very few places to stay other than private homes. A car is a necessity here. The town is dry, so bring your own alcoholic beverages.

The Bayberry Inn
Old Courthouse Road
North Tisbury (Box 546, Vineyard Haven)
(508) 693–1984
Open year-round. Bed and breakfast. Moderate.

Tucked away in a meadow just off the State Road in North Tisbury, the inn is the essence of a small, antique-filled New England bed and breakfast spot. The five bedrooms are spacious, with bright flowered wallpapers and antique furnishings. The paneled dining room, with its fireplace and nineteenth-century ambience, opens onto a charming terrace where a full complimentary breakfast of blueberry waffles, gingerbread pancakes, or other specialties is served. Horses graze in an adjoining field. Afternoon tea is also available. Beaches, tennis, and horseback riding are nearby. Bring your own alcoholic beverages.

The Cove House
Off State Road (P.O. Box 25)
(508) 693–9199
Open year-round. Inexpensive.

These seven one-bedroom apartments located on the south side of the island near the center of West Tisbury are convenient places for a family to stay. Bright and tidy, each unit has a living room with sofa bed, kitchen, bedroom, full bath, and porch. Set in a quiet, rural area with lots of grounds around the building, this is a fine place for children. There's also a pond with a dock for guests to use, and beach passes are provided. The apartments are available for a minimum of three days.

Lambert's Cove Inn
Lambert's Cove Road (RFD, Box 422, Vineyard Haven)
(508) 693–2298
Open year-round. Bed and breakfast. Moderate.

A winding drive through a grove of tall pines reminiscent of northern New England leads to one of the island's superior inns, which measures up to one's expectations in every way: ambience, decor, food, and a gracious country setting. The original part of the house was built in 1790 and greatly enlarged in the 1920s with a barn and carriage house. These have been converted into lovely rooms with bright, colorful wallpapers, country curtains, and antique and wicker furnishings. There are thirteen rooms in all. Many rooms in the outbuildings have their own porches, and one has a small, original greenhouse that has been made into a delightful sitting room with white wicker furniture. The large, comfortable living room in the main building is exceptionally attractive and opens onto the porch. The spacious lawns and lilac, boxwood, and wisteria perfectly complement the surroundings.

In the summer season a full breakfast is served to the inn guests, and in the off-season a continental breakfast is included, or guests may pay for a full breakfast. Guests may order picnic lunches (in insulated containers). The dining room is open to the general public for dinner and Sunday brunch. Bring your own alcoholic beverages. There's one tennis court, and beach passes to the two West Tisbury beaches are provided.

CHILMARK

Having your own means of transportation is a must if you stay in Chilmark. Distances are great to the beaches, restaurants, or grocers, and it's a half-hour drive to the Down-Island towns. There are few places to stay other than private homes. The Chilmark Community Center at Beetlebung Corner is the one gathering place. Like West Tisbury, Chilmark is a dry town.

Breakfast at Tiasquam
Off Middle Road
(508) 645–3685
Open year-round. Bed and breakfast. Moderate.

If you really want to be secluded, but only a fifteen-minute drive to beach or town, this delightful inn hidden in the woods is ideal. There are eight light, airy rooms, half with shared baths. There's a deck where one can have a full, complimentary breakfast in the sun-dappled shade of large oak and beech trees.

There's a rental car available, and beach passes are complimentary, but no smoking or pets are allowed in the building. Bring your own alcoholic beverages.

The Captain Flanders House
North Road
(508) 645–3123
March–November. Bed and breakfast. Inexpensive.

A dirt driveway off the North Road, just above Menemsha, leads past open fields and a windmill and through a stone gateway to this late-seventeenth-century farmhouse built by Captain Richard Flanders, a whaling captain. With views of rolling fields edged with stone walls and a pond down in a valley, it is an attractive, quiet, informal farmhouse setting—one that invites the same guests to return year after year. On the pond there appear to be two dollhouses. These are duck-nesting boxes built by a man who formerly owned the place and are replicas of two historic Edgartown houses. Breakfast is served in an enclosed sun porch. Bring your own alcoholic beverages. Beach passes are provided.

MENEMSHA

Menemsha Inn and Cottages
North Road
(508) 645–2521
April–October. Expensive.

A dirt road leads off the highway just above Menemsha to this inn, which has a marvelous view of Vineyard Sound. There are thirteen efficiency cabins on a hillside that stretches down through the meadows and woods to the beach along the north shore. It is a camplike setting, but the cabins are bright and colorful with fresh paint, crisp curtains, and scatter rugs. They are fully equipped housekeeping units (with the exception of linens). Maid service is provided for those who stay more than a week. Each cabin has its own screened porch, picnic table, outdoor grill, and outdoor shower. The inn also has suites and rooms in the main building. They have their own tennis court, and beach passes are provided. A continental breakfast is served. Bring your own alcoholic beverages.

Beach Plum Inn
North Road
(508) 645–9454
Seasonal. Expensive.

Another dirt road near the Menemsha Inn driveway leads through the woods to this turn-of-the-century house perched on a bluff overlooking Vineyard Sound. An island institution in an eight-acre setting of fields and woodlands, it has, for years, been known for both its excellent gourmet food and distinguished guests. The four guest rooms in the main house and four cottages on the grounds (available by the week) have been a relaxing refuge for prominent individuals in government, business, and the arts.

They serve delicious breakfasts and dinners and provide passes to the local beaches. Bring your own alcoholic beverages.

GAY HEAD

The Outermost Inn
Rural Route 1, Box 271
Lighthouse Road
Expensive.
(508) 645–3511

Located on the high, rolling moors at the western tip of the island, the inn is surrounded by spectacular views of blue sea everywhere: Vineyard Sound, the Rhode Island shoreline, the great sweep of the Atlantic Ocean along the south shore. You also can see Gay Head's historic lighthouse. The seven rooms with private baths have a rustic charm, with unpainted furniture in the warm colors of natural woods highlighted by white walls. The large dining room with fireplace looks seaward, as does every room.

They serve a full complimentary breakfast. A delicious dinner (open to the public by reservation) is available Thursdays through Sundays. Guests can have cocktails on the porch while enjoying those incredible sunsets, and the familiar sound of a recording by one of the Taylors wafts from the living room, where musical instruments crowd in a corner. Hugh Taylor, the inn's owner, is one of the singing Taylors, along with James, Livingston, and Kate. Hugh is also an accomplished sailor, and guests can sign up for day sails to Cuttyhunk Island on his 50-foot catamaran. His wife, Jeannie, whose great-great-grandfather was born at the lighthouse, devotes full time to running this unique hideaway. A car is a necessity, except for the short walk to the beach and the concessions at the Gay Head cliffs. Bring your own alcoholic beverages.

CAMPGROUNDS AND YOUTH HOSTEL

Martha's Vineyard Family Campground
Edgartown–Vineyard Haven Road
Vineyard Haven
In season, (508) 693–3772; off-season, (617) 784–3615
May–October.

This campground, located one mile from Vineyard Haven center, is nestled in a grove of oak trees. It accommodates 180 vehicles. The campground allows one motor vehicle, one large tent, or two small tents per site. There is a recreation hall with table tennis, billiards, and other activities, a playground, a ball field, a camp store, bike rentals, and other facilities. They charge $15 per day for a campsite for two (including electricity and water hookups), and $18 per day for a trailer site for two (including electricity, water, and sewer). No dogs or motorcycles are allowed. Additional adults are $7 per person per day.

Webb's Camping Area
Barnes Road, Oak Bluffs (RFD 2, Box 100, Vineyard Haven, MA
    02568)
(508) 693–0233
May–September.

Winding through a scenic grove of pine trees, this ninety-acre site offers swimming and fishing on Lagoon Pond. It has a recreational hall, general store, bikes for rent, dumping station, showers, laundry, and play yard for children. No pets, motorcycles, or trail bikes.

There are 150 large, wooded sites. The charge is $18 a night for two adults, or $126 per week. Tent sites are $16 a night, or $112 a week. There's a separate area for cyclists and backpackers.

Youth Hostel
West Tisbury Road, West Tisbury
(508) 693–2665
Seasonal.

Two of West Tisbury's leading citizens, the late Daniel and Lillian Manter, gave this building to the town for a youth hostel. It provides dormitory sleeping and cooking facilities for bicyclists and hikers. The maximum length of stay is three days in summer and longer in the fall and spring. Space is at a premium, so it is best to make a reservation. Members pay $10 per night per person; non-members pay $13 per night per person.

7

WHERE
TO EAT

There is a wide variety of eating places on the Vineyard to suit all tastes and preferences. You'll find elegant and expensive restaurants as well as simple family restaurants, plus many places to get a take-out snack or lunch for a day on the beach or bicycling around the island. Many places are open from the spring through the fall; all Up-Island places are closed in the winter.

You may find the less-expensive places quite crowded during the busiest time of midsummer, so it's advisable to plan ahead if possible. Some of the more-expensive places prefer that you make a reservation. Proprietors at the expensive restaurants prefer to have their guests appropriately dressed, with the men in jackets and the women in dressy slacks or dresses; this is particularly true in Edgartown, which is more formal than the other towns. Be sure to inquire about payment when making a reservation; some restaurants only take certain credit cards, and others won't accept personal checks.

The general price range for the various places listed in this book is as follows: expensive, $20 to $35 per entree; moderate, $10 to $20; and inexpensive, $5 to $10. A moderate to expensive range usually means that the lunch is moderate in cost while the dinner might be $20 or more; inexpensive to moderate implies the same kind of price variation. These prices will vary a bit, depending on the extras one might order, and all are subject to fluctuations in the market prices for lobster and swordfish.

Shucking scallops for a wonderful dinner.

EDGARTOWN

The Square Rigger
Upper Main Street
627-9968
Expensive.

This old house at the fork in the road on Upper Main Street has been a restaurant for years. It has a tavern ambience with its plain wood tables, captains' chairs, old beams, and a long bar.

It is known for the delicious steak and seafood specialties that are charbroiled on an open hearth. Owned by the same person who owns the famous Homeport in Menemsha, the lobster choices are exceptional. Dinner nightly from 6 P.M. Handicapped access. Open year-round.

Andrea's Restaurant
Upper Main Street
627-5850
Moderate to expensive.

For those who love northern Italian cuisine, Andrea's is very good indeed. It is located in an old, white clapboard house on Main Street, two blocks from the center of town. There's a charming, white, latticed terrace for outdoor dining or a cellar cocktail lounge for drinks before dinner. The green and white dining room with ceiling fans seats about thirty-five and isn't crowded. The service here is prompt and friendly. The choices are tempting: pasta dishes; Sirloin Cardinale done with peppercorns, flambéed with brandy, and topped with a special house sauce; or Lobster Andrea, with vegetables and lobster baked in phyllo dough and served with a cream sauce, plus other unusual entrees. The desserts are equally delicious, and everything is a la carte. Dinner is the only meal served, and the restaurant is open from Easter to October. Reservations are suggested. Handicapped access. Ample parking.

Beeftender Restaurant
Upper Main Street
627-8344
Moderate.

As the name implies, beef is prepared in many different ways in this casual, no-frills restaurant with a friendly atmosphere. They also serve swordfish and lobster as well as a nightly seafood special. There is a very good salad bar, and the pleasant cocktail lounge has a delicious seafood bar. The restaurant is open year-round for dinner. Handicapped access. Ample parking.

Savoir Fare
Post Office Square
627–9864
Moderate.

This bright little luncheonette, with its metal umbrella tables in a garden setting, gives no clue to the fact that it is also a superb caterer.

The lunch food is excellent. They also serve full dinners and light a la carte selections and were recommended by *Gourmet Magazine*. Beer and wine available. Closed midwinter.

L'etoile
South Summer Street
627–5187
Expensive.

L'etoile, in the Charlotte Inn, is one of the island's premier restaurants. The pleasant art gallery setting is enhanced by its indoor terrace and outdoor garden with an attractive fountain, flowers, and cool green plantings. It is the ideal background for excellent French nouvelle cuisine. One delicious specialty of the restaurant is roasted Norwegian salmon filet with a horseradish and ginger crust. The wines are excellent, and everything is beautifully served.

The restaurant serves lunch and dinner daily in season and on weekends in the winter months. Reservations are necessary. Handicapped access is available.

Starbuck's
North Water Street
627–7000
Moderate.

The turn-of-the-century Harborview Hotel is a treasure. Its dining room, Starbuck's, has a sweeping view of the Edgartown Lighthouse and the entrance to Edgartown Harbor. There is a cafe next to the dining room where a piano player adds just the right nostalgic touch. Guests can have cocktails out on the porch, sitting in rush-seated rocking chairs while they enjoy watching ships sail into the harbor at sunset. The restaurant has the usual selection of native seafood— swordfish, lobster, sole, and quahog chowder—as well as lamb, duckling, and veal. Reservations are required, and men must wear jackets. Breakfast, lunch, and dinner are served year-round, and their weekly buffets have been famous for half a century. Handicapped access is available. Ample parking.

The Newes
Kelly Street
627–4394
Moderate.

The eighteenth-century tavern-like character with the exposed original old beams and brick walls makes this Kelly House hotel pub a delightful spot for a light lunch or dinner. Located in the center of town, it's adjacent to, but not on, the harbor. The clam chowder, salads, lobster rolls, and other familiar choices are quite tasty. Open year-round from 11:00 A.M. to 11:00 P.M. daily. Handicapped access. No reservations required.

Navigator Room and Boathouse Bar
Foot of Main Street
627–4320
Inexpensive to moderate.

Right on the harbor, with a great water view, the Boathouse Bar has more maritime atmosphere than any other restaurant in Edgartown. The old, exposed beams are hung with ships' lights, wooden blocks, harpoons, fishnets, and lobster buoys. There's a long bar at one end of the room, a lovely patio outside for luncheon in good weather, and on cool spring and fall days a fire blazes in the freestanding fireplace. Both their special hamburger and their croissant filled with Seafood Newburg are very good. Handicapped access is available.

Upstairs is the Navigator Room with a more expansive view of the sailboats and motorboats moving through Edgartown Harbor. It is a slightly more formal atmosphere than the Boathouse Bar, and the menu is a little more expensive. Lunch and dinner are served in season, and only dinner is served after Labor Day. Both the Navigator Room and the Boathouse Bar are closed in the winter. Reservations are unnecessary, but both dining rooms are popular.

Shiretown Inn
North Water Street
627–3353
Expensive.

The tavern-like dining room in the Daggett House in Edgartown dates back to the seventeenth century.

One of the island's most charming restaurants is in the Shiretown Inn, 2 blocks from the center of town. Located in a quiet garden setting in the back of the inn, the large dining room adjoins a covered terrace dining area. The dining room's colorful flowered wallpaper, complemented by soft pink tablecloths and fresh flowers, sets the tone for this delightful indoor-outdoor dining spot. Guests can have a pre-dinner cocktail in the pub adjacent to the dining room or out in the garden.

The menu, from local seafood specialties and delicious clam and quahog chowder to Veal Scallopini Maison, is excellent. Freshly made specialties for dessert are prepared daily in the bakery.

Dinner is the only meal served, and reservations are required. The service is courteous and cordial, and there is parking in the rear for guests. Handicapped access is available. The restaurant is open from early spring to late fall.

Lattanzi's
Post Office Square
627–8854
Inexpensive to moderate.

This charming, seasonal restaurant tucked away behind the courthouse is a real delight. The antique reproductions are elegant. Queen Anne chairs, mahogany tables, brass fixtures, lovely china, and fresh flowers create an ambience matched by the exceptional cuisine and courteous service. The restaurant is well known for its excellent wines, special coffees, mouth-watering desserts, and fish specialties, and it is open for dinner. Reservations are recommended, and handicapped access is available.

OAK BLUFFS

Lola's
Beach Road
693–5007
Moderate.

There are two restaurants in the building adjacent to The Island Inn: Lola's and the Bluefish Lounge. The former is a large, indoor eatery with a salad bar, and its specialties are southern seafood and char-grilled entrees; the restaurant serves dinner only, year-round. the Bluefish Lounge is the casual, lighter pub menu. Dinner is served year-round, both on the attractive patio and inside. They have tasty grilled fish, and a children's menu. Full bar. Ample parking and handicapped access.

The Oyster Bar
Circuit Avenue
693–3300
Moderate.

The decor is inviting in this restaurant with its fine linens and courteous service. The delicious cuisine is one of the island's best. The chef, who has published his own cookbook, is highly imaginative, and choices include charcoal-grilled calamari, quail and polenta, deviled crab, and Chinese red-cooked snapper. The menu is large and features many creative fish entrees. The restaurant is open seasonally; inquire about the fall and spring schedule. Full bar. Handicapped access.

David's Island House
Circuit Avenue
693–4516
Inexpensive to moderate.

Established in 1978 by well-known, blind, concert pianist David Crohan, Island House guests are treated to his delightful classical music and popular improvisations nightly during and after dinner. The cocktail lounge/piano bar is open every night. The food is good here, and three meals a day are served, beginning at 8:30 in the morning. There is the usual selection of seafood and meat entrees, chowders, and David's own special bouillabaisse. The restaurant is open May through September. Handicapped access.

Giordano's
Circuit Avenue
693–0184
Inexpensive.

An excellent place to go for pizza in Oak Bluffs, Giordano's also has a restaurant, a clam bar, and a thriving take-out section. They have a large menu and serve American and Italian dishes and arguably the best fried clams on the island. They are located across from the Flying Horses carousel and are open on a seasonal basis. Handicapped access.

Linda Jean's Restaurant
Circuit Avenue
693–4093
Inexpensive.

This small, simple family restaurant serves good homemade food. It is especially pleasing to early risers, as it is open from 6:00 A.M. to 8:00 P.M. seven days a week. A favorite dinner here is the seafood platter with French fries, coleslaw, rolls, and butter. Takeout available. Open year-round. Handicapped access.

Ocean View Restaurant and Cocktail Lounge
Chapman Avenue
693–2207
Inexpensive to moderate.

This favorite year-round family restaurant is located near the harbor. It is paneled and has square wooden tables, and there is a nice tavern room. The food is good, with many island fish selections. During the off-season they have a Wednesday night lobster special, which is very popular. Lunch and dinner are served daily, and reservations are required for six or more guests. Handicapped access is available, and there is plenty of parking space.

Papa's Pizza
Circuit Avenue
693–1400
Inexpensive.

Butcher-block tables with long wooden benches and old photographs of Oak Bluffs decorate this popular pizza parlor. There is a large pizza selection here, one of the favorites being Papa John's Special with cheese, onion, mushrooms, sausage, and green peppers. Submarine sandwiches are also featured, including the popular Steak Sub Bomb. Beer and wine are served. It is open daily all year for lunch and dinner.

VINEYARD HAVEN

The Black Dog Tavern
Beach Road
693–9223
Inexpensive to moderate.

The only restaurant on the harbor, the Black Dog Tavern has a weatherbeaten eighteenth-century charm with old ceiling beams and plain wooden tables; a screened porch overlooks the beach. It is located next to the steamship wharf. An island landmark, it is very popular and can be crowded at times. It serves reasonably priced, good food, using local seafood and fresh island vegetables; the pastries are superb. It is open daily from 6:00 A.M. to 10:00 P.M. year-round. No reservations are accepted. Bring your own alcoholic beverages if you wish.

Louis' Tisbury Cafe
State Road
693–3255
Inexpensive.

About a mile out of Vineyard Haven on the State Road, this plain, brown-shingled building gives no clue as to the quality of the food, which is very good.

The front room is a take-out delicatessen open at noon, and the back room with its round wooden tables is the dining area, open from 5:30 to 9:00 P.M. daily, year-round.

Their pasta is made fresh daily, the hot and cold subs are delicious, and their most popular entree is shrimp sautéed in garlic butter and tossed with pasta in a tomato cream sauce. You may bring your own alcoholic beverages.

The Black Dog Tavern on Vineyard Haven harbor.

Borderlands
Main Street
693–8087
Inexpensive to moderate.

Conveniently located just a block from the ferry, the former La Patis-
serie now serves its regular delicious croissants for breakfast, light
lunches, and native Southwestern cuisine for dinner. Owned by the superb chef of Le Grenier, it now features Santa Fe Seafood Stew, Enchi-
ladas Verdes, Burritos, and other original entrees. Open daily both
indoors and out on a sidewalk terrace. No reservations are accepted.
Bring your own alcoholic beverages.

Le Grenier French Restaurant
Main Street
693–4906
Moderate to expensive.

Vineyard Haven's premier restaurant, and one of the island's absolute
best. The chef and owner, from Lyon, France, is imaginative and cre-
ates delicate and delicious country French food. The unusual selections on the large menu include quail with grapes and raspberries and
venison with black currant sauce, which are elegant and not found in
the other island restaurants. The room seats ninety, and the pastel
linens, candlelit tables, and skylights provide an attractive atmosphere.
Dinner and Sunday brunch are the only meals served here. Located
upstairs above Borderlands, it is open year-round except for a short period during midwinter, and reservations are required. You may bring
your own alcoholic beverages.

Tisbury Inn Cafe
Main Street
693–3416
Moderate.

The Tisbury Inn Cafe is located in the center of town; there are sidewalk tables out front. The decor is plain Jane, but the food is good. The
chef makes his own pastas and rolls, and the chocolate desserts are famous. Half-portions for light eaters are offered. The restaurant is open
daily for breakfast, lunch, and dinner year-round. Reservations are suggested only for dinner. You may bring your own alcoholic beverages.

WEST TISBURY

Lambert's Cove Inn
Lambert's Cove Road
693–2298
Moderate.

This charming country inn, which has two dining rooms and an attractive porch looking out on an old apple orchard, has been featured in *Gourmet Magazine*. The dinner selections include lamb, beef, veal, and fish. Their excellent Coquilles St. Jacques is made with local scallops, and the fresh Norwegian salmon is particularly delicious. Both the porch and the large dining room are relaxed and comfortable places to gather before going in to dinner. Their superb Sunday brunch, served from 10:30 A.M. to 2:00 P.M., has become an island tradition, particularly in the off-season. Dinner is served daily in the summer, and on weekends during the rest of the year. Reservations are requested. Bring your own alcoholic beverages.

NORTH TISBURY

The Red Cat
State Road
693–9599
Moderate.

This luncheonette, Humphrey's Bakery next door (which serves coffee and delicious baked goods), and CJ Cafe sandwich shop are the only eating places in North Tisbury.

Fresh, simple seafood and homemade soups are popular, and the take-out counter is handy for those on their way to the beach. They're open for lunch and dinner seasonally; closed Sundays. Bring your own alcoholic beverages.

MENEMSHA

Homeport
Menemsha
645–2679
Moderate.

Overlooking Menemsha Creek, which runs from the harbor into Menemsha Pond, this casual eating place has been known for its fresh seafood for years. Especially popular are the chowder, the fish platter of fried shrimp, whitefish, scallops, and oysters, and the boiled lobster and stuffed quahog. For years people from the Down-Island towns have brought their cocktails to drink out on the stone jetty or Menemsha Beach and then enjoyed a seafood dinner at Homeport. Open on a seasonal basis for dinner only, and reservations are necessary. Handicapped access is available.

Beach Plum Inn
Menemsha
645–9454
Expensive.

Hidden away in a lovely setting overlooking Vineyard Sound, this island landmark is one of the top restaurants for dinner. The seating is limited and reservations are required, but the cuisine is so exceptional, it's well worth finding your way here.

They have their own vegetable garden, and the menu changes daily. The desserts are sinful and sensational. Open May to October. Alcoholic beverages may be brought to the restaurant.

CHILMARK

The Feast of Chilmark
Beetlebung Corner
645–3553
Expensive.

Located in the center of Chilmark, this is a favorite dinner spot for Up-Island vacationers. It has a relaxed atmosphere with spacious seating, contemporary furniture, and art-decorated walls. The local lamb and fish entrees are delicious, while the Seafood Marinara with lobster, shrimp, scallops, and littlenecks over linguni is the most popular.

There is a separate take-out section where homemade pastries and coffee are available in the morning. While it is not open for lunch, the restaurant is available for private parties any time. Open May to October. Reservations suggested. Bring your own alcoholic beverages.

GAY HEAD

The Aquinnah Shop
At the cliffs
645–9654
Inexpensive.

This restaurant and gift shop at the tip of the Gay Head Cliffs is something of an island institution. Opened in 1949, the shop was bought by Ann and Luther Madison in 1969, and three of their children work here with them. The family is steeped in island tradition: Luther's father, Napoleon Bonaparte Madison, was a well-known, highly respected member of the Gay Head Indian tribe.

One of the island's most popular attractions, the cliffs are a major stopping point for the busloads of daily tourists. According to Ann

The Elizabeth Islands, which can be seen across Vineyard Sound, are visible from the porch of the Outermost Inn, located on the high, rolling moors on the western tip of the island.

Madison, sixteen buses arrive at once at lunchtime, so her three take-out windows and inside tables are swamped. If you can, it's best to visit the area at another time.

The restaurant's open porch, which hangs on the edge of the cliffs, offers a striking view of Norman's Land Island to the left, and Cutty-hunk, the outermost of the Elizabeth Island chain, to the right.

The restaurant's quahog chowder is made with local clams only, and the fishburgers and lobster rolls are delicious. Ann's pies are highly popular, and many people order whole pies a day in advance. The restaurant opens Easter morning for a sunrise service on the cliffs and closes in October. Handicapped access is available.

FAMILY RESTAURANTS

Finding an inexpensive or moderately priced restaurant suitable for restless young children can be a problem. The following list, however, should be helpful. Some of these restaurants also are listed earlier in this chapter.

EDGARTOWN

Carolina's
Upper Main Street
627–8857
Inexpensive.

This simple spot, where you eat off picnic tables, features southern bar-beque as well as hamburgers and sandwiches. Ample parking. Wine and beer available. Open for lunch and dinner. Handicapped access. Seasonal. Take out.

Savoir Fare
Post Office Square
627–9864
Moderate.

The food is absolutely superb in this quiet, patio garden setting just off Main Street. Open for lunch and dinner until 9:00 P.M. They have take-out and are premier caterers. Beer and wine are served. Ample parking. Closed midwinter. Handicapped access.

The Wharf
Foot of Main Street
627–9966
Inexpensive.

Lunch and dinner are served on this glass-enclosed porch adjacent to the Edgartown waterfront. Its fine, light fare includes soups, salads, sandwiches, and fish and beef entrees as well as a good children's menu. It is a handy waterfront eatery. Seasonal.

Adjacent to it is The Wharf Pub, a sports bar, which is a popular spot with young people and open all winter.

OAK BLUFFS

Linda Jean's Restaurant
Circuit Avenue
693–4093
Inexpensive.

A favorite of island residents, the homemade food here is fine: hamburgers, sandwiches, and desserts children enjoy. A favorite of adults is the seafood platter. Open 6:00 A.M. to 8:00 P.M. daily year-round. Bring your own alcoholic beverages.

Mike's Bar and Grill
Beach Road
693–3330
Inexpensive.

Adjacent to Anthony's Restaurant at the Island Inn, Mike's patio has colorful umbrellas facing a golf course and is an attractive setting for casual dining. The raw bar is excellent, the seafood is delicious, and the soups and sandwiches are fine for children. Open year-round from 7:00 A.M. to 11:00 P.M. Full bar. Ample parking. Handicapped access.

Papa's Pizza
Circuit Avenue
693–1400
Inexpensive.

A spaghetti and pizza paradise for youngsters, this restaurant has an informal ambience. Tavern tables and old photographs line the walls.

It's a favorite of islanders. Beer and wine are served. Open year-round for lunch and dinner; takeout is available.

Ocean View Restaurant
Chapman Avenue
693–2207
Inexpensive to moderate.

This is a popular year-round restaurant located near the harbor in an open field, where restless children can romp while waiting to be served. The fine food includes many fish selections. Lunch and dinner daily. Full bar. Handicapped access. Ample parking.

VINEYARD HAVEN

Portside
Beach Road
693–5580
Inexpensive.

This roadside stand located next to the Lagoon Bridge has a lot to recommend it. The picnic tables overlook the lagoon, and the hamburgers, hot dogs, and fish sandwiches are delicious. A fun spot for children. Seasonal.

Chang's Chinese Restaurant
State Road
693–8500
Inexpensive.

Located on the State Road just beyond Cronig's Market, this quiet little restaurant under the Vineyard Electronics Store is ideal for young and old. There's a walled-in flagstone terrace for outdoor meals and a bright interior with small tables. The homemade food is very good and includes Chinese food and a children's menu. Ample parking. Open year-round daily for breakfast, lunch, and dinner, Thursday through Sunday. Bring your own alcoholic beverages.

Louis' Tisbury Cafe
State Road
693–3255
Moderate.

Char-grilled seafood and other delicious barbecues are favorites for the many island residents who frequent this year-round restaurant. The cafe is also known for its fine Italian food. Located across from Cronig's Market, there is ample parking in the rear. They serve lunch and dinner, and also have take-out. Bring alcoholic beverages if you wish.

The Black Dog Tavern
Beach Street Extension
693–9223
Moderate to expensive.

Restless children can play on the beach until meals are served in this well-known eatery on the Vineyard Haven waterfront. The creatively prepared entrees are delicious, with particular emphasis on local fish, and there's a nice array of simple selections for children. Open year-round for breakfast, lunch, and dinner, the latter served from 5 P.M. to 10 P.M. Bring your own alcoholic beverages.

NORTH TISBURY

The Red Cat
State Road
693–9599
Inexpensive.

One of the few spots in the mid-island area for lunch and dinner, this roadside restaurant has hearty, home-cooked food; the chili and fresh seafood are particularly good. The picnic tables are convenient for youngsters. There is ample parking. Closed Sundays but otherwise open until 10:00 P.M. Bring your own alcoholic beverages. Open seasonally.

MENEMSHA

Homeport
645–2679
Moderate.

An old island favorite famous for its seafood, Homeport is open for dinner nightly during the season. It has become so popular that reservations are required. Both the patio and dining room look out across Menemsha Pond. Bring alcoholic beverages if you wish. Ample parking. Handicapped access.

The Martha's Vineyard Deli
Basin Road
645–9902
Inexpensive.

There are tasty soups, salads, sandwiches, and desserts that can be picked up here to take to the beach or to enjoy on the premises. Bring your own alcoholic beverages. Seasonal.

GAY HEAD

The Aquinnah Shop
Gay Head Cliffs
645–9654
Inexpensive.

This island landmark, with its breathtaking view from the tip of the cliffs, serves delicious food: homemade pies, chowders, sandwiches, popular fishburgers, and what one gourmet from San Francisco called "the finest, sweetest lobster I've ever eaten anywhere." It does get very crowded at noontime when the tour buses stop. Open for breakfast, lunch, and dinner in the summer; only breakfast and lunch are served in the spring and fall. Handicapped access. Bring your own alcoholic beverages.

8

TELEPHONE NUMBERS & ADDRESSES

Here are some important telephone numbers and addresses for your basic needs during your island vacation or to answer your questions before you visit the island.

General

For *emergency* only—fire, police, or ambulance, dial 911
Martha's Vineyard Hospital, Linton Lane, Oak Bluffs, 693–0410
Massachusetts MSPCA, Vineyard Haven Road, Edgartown, 627–8662
Animal Health Care, Martha's Vineyard Airport, 693–6515
Massachusetts State Police, Temihigan Avenue, Oak Bluffs, 693–0545
Chilmark Police Headquarters, Beetlebung Corner, 645–3310
Edgartown Police Headquarters, Church Street, 627–4343
Gay Head Police Headquarters, State Road, Chilmark, 645–9978
Oak Bluffs Police Headquarters, Oak Bluffs Avenue (ferry wharf), 696–4240
Vineyard Haven (Tisbury) Police Headquarters, Beach Road parking lot, 693–0474
West Tisbury Police Headquarters, State Road, 693–0020
U.S. Coast Guard, Menemsha Station, 645–2611
Weather Forecast, 1–771–5522
Dukes County Court House, Edgartown, 627–3751

Churches

Edgartown

Edgartown United Methodist Church (Old Whaling Church), Main Street, 645–3100
Faith Community Church, Meeting House Way, 693–4031
Federated Church, South Summer Street, 627–4421
St. Andrew's Episcopal Church, North Summer Street, 627–5330
St. Elizabeth's Roman Catholic Church, Main Street, 627–5017

Oak Bluffs

Apostolic House of Prayer, Pequot Avenue, 693–8485
Our Lady Star of the Sea, Circuit Avenue, 693–0342

The West Tisbury Congregational Church.

The ivy-covered Saint Andrew's Episcopal Church in Edgartown was built in 1899.

Seventh Day Adventists, Cottagers Building (no telephone)
The Tabernacle, Camp Ground (no telephone)
Trinity Episcopal Church, East Chop Drive, 693–3780
Trinity United Methodist Church, Camp Ground, 693–0589
Union Chapel, Circuit Avenue 693–2426

Vineyard Haven

Assembly of God, State Road, 693–4622
First Baptist Church, Spring Street, 693–1539
Grace Episcopal Church, Woodlawn Avenue, 693–0332
Jehovah's Witnesses, Pine Tree Road, 693–3931
Martha's Vineyard Hebrew Center, Centre Street, 693–0745 or 693–1239
Methodist Church, Church Street, 693–0476
St. Augustine's Roman Catholic Rectory, Franklin Street, 693–0103
The Unitarian Universalist Society of Martha's Vineyard, Main Street,
    693–8982

West Tisbury

First Congregational Church, West Tisbury Center, 693–2842
United Methodist Church, Lambert's Cove Road, 693–0476

Chilmark

Chilmark United Methodist Church, Menemsha Crossroads, 645–3100

Gay Head

Community Baptist Church, Gay Head center, 693–1539

Conservation Organizations

There are now seven nonprofit conservation organizations on the island. Each emphasizes a different function, but all of them are concerned with protecting and enhancing the natural beauty of the island.
They are the Martha's Vineyard Garden Club, Sheriff's Meadow Foundation, Trustees of Reservations, Vineyard Conservation Society, Vineyard Open Land Foundation, Massachusetts Audubon Society, and
Martha's Vineyard Land Bank, which manages the proceeds from a 2
percent tax on all real estate transactions to acquire farms, beaches,
and woodlands for the public benefit. With the exception of the Land
Bank in Edgartown and the Audubon Society, which is located at the
Felix Neck Wildlife Sanctuary, their offices are at the Mary P. Wakeman
Conservation Center on Lambert's Cove Road. Anyone wishing to make
a contribution, financial or otherwise, should contact these groups.

Information, General

The Martha's Vineyard Chamber of Commerce is helpful in answering
general questions about the island. It is located on Beach Road in Vineyard Haven, 2 blocks from the ferry wharf. The telephone number is
(508) 693–0085. If you are writing to them, use the Beach Road address, Vineyard Haven, MA 02568.

The Edgartown Visitors' Center, located across Church Street from
the back of the Old Whaling Church, is another valuable resource. You

can find public restrooms and a post office here in addition to important travel information. Shuttle buses from Vineyard Haven and Oak Bluffs terminate here, as do several chartered bus tours.

Information, Historical

The Vineyard Museum, on School Street in Edgartown, is the island's main museum. The staff there are helpful in answering questions about the Vineyard's history, as well as genealogical queries. The museum also publishes an excellent historical quarterly, *The Intelligencer,* which is on sale at their offices along with other publications on the history of the Vineyard. Financial contributions are always welcome, should any visitor care to subscribe to the quarterly or give directly to the museum. The telephone number is 627–4441.

Libraries

Chilmark Public Library, Chilmark Center, 645–3360
Edgartown Public Library, North Water Street, 627–4221
Gale Huntington Library, Vineyard Museum, School Street, Edgartown, 627–4441
Gay Head Public Library, Gay Head Center, 645–9552
Oak Bluffs Public Library, Circuit Avenue, 693–9433
Vineyard Haven Public Library, Main Street, 696–4211
West Tisbury Public Library, South Road, 693–3366

Museums

The Vineyard Museum, School Street, Edgartown, 627–4441
Old Schoolhouse Museum, Main Street, Vineyard Haven, 693–3860
Cottage Museum, Campground, Oak Bluffs

U.S. Post Offices and Zip Codes

Chilmark, Beetlebung Corner, 645–2535, zip 02535
Edgartown, Upper Main Street, 627–7318, zip 02539
Gay Head (Chilmark post office and zip code)
Menemsha, 645–3501, zip 02552 (open May 15–September 15)
Oak Bluffs, Park Avenue, 693–1049, zip 02557
Vineyard Haven, Lagoon Pond Road, 693–2818, zip 02568
West Tisbury, State Road, North Tisbury and West Tisbury, 693–7899,
    zip 02575

9

LEISURE
ACTIVITIES

Antique Shops

Browsing in antique shops is a favorite pastime for many island visitors. You will find antiques and collectibles for sale in all the towns, except Gay Head. The prices and quality vary a great deal, from simple collectibles to country pine furniture, china, early American brasses, turn-of-the-century wicker, and nineteenth-century furniture and reproductions.

Art Galleries

There are many art galleries in the island towns featuring photographs and paintings. Island scenes in watercolors and prints predominate, but the variety is enormous, from the least-expensive lighthouse print to works by well-known artists whose work has been featured in art galleries located in New York, Boston, and other urban art centers.

Art Instruction

The Old Sculpin Art Gallery in Edgartown has been offering art lessons to both children and adults during the summer months for many years. Classes are given upstairs in the gallery building on Dock Street next to the Chappaquiddick Ferry Dock. For details, telephone 627–4881. The Nathan Mayhew Seminars has a workshop in painting and drawing for adults, with a three-week session in July and a two-week session in August. Children's art classes also are offered. Call 693–6603 for more details. The institution is located on North William Street in Vineyard Haven.

Beaches

The island beaches are very popular with summer and fall visitors. The gently lapping waves all along the north and northeast Sound side of the island are ideal for swimming or launching a sailboard. Some of these beaches are pebbly, while others are wide and sandy. The Atlantic Ocean beaches have very fine sand in most places and coarse sand in others. The size of the surf depends on the weather conditions. Many beaches are open to the general public, but a number of town beaches are open to residents and guests only.

Chappaquiddick

Cape Pogue Wildlife Refuge and Wasque Reservation are two adjoining beaches on Chappaquiddick Island that run along the east side of the island. They are managed by the Trustees of Reservations and are subject to their regulations. To reach the beach take the Chappy ferry and go directly across the island on the only paved road that later becomes a dirt road and leads to the Wasque parking lot. The beach is open to all.

Edgartown

The Lighthouse Beach is at the entrance to Edgartown Harbor, by the lighthouse, and is open to all.

The Katama Beach, the public beach at South Beach, is on the south side of Edgartown. There is a shuttle bus to the beach from the center of town. If you drive here, follow Pease Point Way to the beach, which is 3 miles from town. It is an extremely popular, 3-mile-long barrier beach. There are lifeguards in certain areas; however, there are no toilet facilities or food stands and visitors are constantly asked to pick up their own trash and not to trample or drive on the dunes. Katama, in Indian dialect, means "crab fishing place."

The Edgartown–Oak Bluffs State Beach (called Joseph A. Sylvia Beach) is a 2-mile stretch of open beach along the State Road that runs between Oak Bluffs and Edgartown. It is a fine swimming beach, with some areas more pebbly than others, and it is very popular in midsummer. There are lifeguards at the Edgartown end of the beach, but like all island beaches there are no food stands, other than an ice cream truck at the Oak Bluffs end, and no toilet facilities. The beach is open to all.

Oak Bluffs

Oak Bluffs Town Beach is a calm, shallow beach with fine sand that runs along either side of the ferry wharf in Oak Bluffs. It is open to all.

Vineyard Haven

Owen Park Beach near the ferry dock on the harbor is a small, sandy beach open to all.

Lake Tashmoo is outside of Vineyard Haven on the north shore. To reach it, you can go out Main Street or Franklin Street, heading toward West Chop. Turn left on Daggett Avenue and follow it to Herring

Low tide and a gentle surf on a summer's day at South Beach.

Creek Road, a dirt road that goes down to the beach. The beach is sandy, there is usually a fair current at the entrance to Vineyard Sound, and it is open to all.

West Tisbury

Long Point Wildlife Refuge is along the Atlantic Ocean and Tisbury Great Pond. It is a 580-acre preserve managed by the Trustees of Reservations. They own a half-mile of South Beach, and swimming, surf fishing, and picnicking are permitted here. There is an admission fee of $2 per person age 15 and over and a charge of $5 per vehicle. There also is a limit of fifty-five cars per day. To reach Long Point take Deep Bottom Road, which is exactly 1 mile west of the entrance to Martha's Vineyard Airport, and follow the signs along this narrow, bumpy dirt road for 3 miles to the refuge. It is open to all.

Lambert's Cove Beach is on the north shore in West Tisbury. Unlike many areas along the shore where the beach is pebbly, here there is fine sand. The beach is for West Tisbury residents and guests only.

Chilmark and Menemsha

Lucy Vincent Beach is on the south shore facing the Atlantic Ocean. There is a lifeguard on duty, but the beach is open to Chilmark residents and guests only.

Squibnocket Beach on the south shore is a sandy, wide, beautiful beach with long, slow rollers coming ashore. It is open to Chilmark residents and guests only.

Menemsha Town Beach is right beside the stone jetty at the entrance to the harbor. It is a slightly pebbly beach open to all, and the water is gentle and calm. No lifeguard or facilities of any kind are available.

Menemsha Hills Reservation is a 200-acre sanctuary with rugged hiking trails leading down to the beach. Off the North Road, midway between Tabor House Road and Menemsha Cross Road, is the parking entrance. No swimming or dogs allowed.

Gay Head

Gay Head Beach is that long stretch of ocean beach you can see from the Gay Head Cliffs, and the road running alongside the beach is called Moshup's Trail. It is open to the public and carefully supervised.

Lobsterville Beach is along the north shore of the island. Because it is a Vineyard Sound beach, the waters are gentle, and the beach is pebbly. All along the road opposite the beach, the low, rolling dunes are a protected tern and gull nesting area. A road here also leads over to Menemsha Pond Beach. This is a public beach, without lifeguard or facilities.

Berry Picking

Each year there are fewer and fewer places to go berry picking on the island. Those residents who do know where to find some blueberries, beach plums, grapes, or wild raspberries are not going to share this information with anyone. However, jam and jellies made locally are available in the gift shops and grocery stores. Thimble farm, located off the inland Edgartown, allows customers to pick their own strawberries and raspberries.

Bicycling

The island is noted for its varied, undulating terrain. There are, however, a few flat spots for easy pedaling. They are the road from Vineyard

Everyone enjoys diving off the bridge at the Edgartown–Oak Bluffs State Beach. (above)

After an active day of playing on the beach, a nap feels just right. (above right)

Anglers try their luck. (right)

Haven to Oak Bluffs and on to Edgartown; a short stretch in mid-island by the airport; and State Road between North Tisbury and Vineyard Haven. The fun of riding around has been greatly improved by the addition of bike paths, which are also safer. Biking through the pines alongside the state forest, out of danger from passing cars, is a delightful ride.

Bird Watching

There are many places to go bird watching on the island. Various groups sponsor bird and nature walks. The Felix Neck Wildlife Sanctuary, which has its own bird walks, also has information about other groups on the island that sponsor walks throughout the year. Call 627–4850 for more information.

Boat Rentals and Instruction

The following places have small boats or sailboards for rent, and they also offer instruction. Check with the chamber of commerce for other rentals.

Edgartown

The Harborside Inn on South Water Street has both outboard motorboats and small sailboats available. They also provide instruction. Call 627–4321.

Oak Bluffs

Dockside Whaler Rentals at Oak Bluffs Harbor has the popluar Boston Whaler for rent. Call 693–8476.

Vineyard Haven

Wind's Up on the Beach Road has sailboards, catamarans, and Sunfish. Instruction is also available. Call 693–4252.

There are larger sailboats that take guests out for a half-day or for private parties. The charter companies vary from year to year, so it's best to check with the shipyards and the newspapers. In Vineyard Haven usually there is a large cruise ship that has evening dinner cruises and advertises in the local papers.

Boat Ramps

For those who have a small boat, it's helpful to know where you can launch it. All the launching ramps are in protected bays and lagoons, but these protected waters lead out to sea for those who want to go off-shore for sailing or fishing.

Boat ramps can be found at the following locations:

Edgartown

Anthier's Landing into Sengekontacket Pond; or Katama, at the south end of Katama Bay Road, into Katama Bay.

Vineyard Haven

Beach Road, on the Vineyard Haven side of the lagoon drawbridge, into the lagoon; or Lake Street into Lake Tashmoo.

Oak Bluffs

East Chop Drive, along the north side of Oak Bluffs Harbor, into the harbor; or Medeiros Cove, on the west side of Oak Bluffs, into the lagoon.

Gay Head

At the Gay Head–Chilmark town line at Hariph's Creek Bridge, into Nashaquitsa Pond; or Lobsterville, across the creek from Menemsha Harbor, into Menemsha Pond.

Bowling

On the State Road in Vineyard Haven is Spinneker Lanes (693–9691), which is particularly popular in the winter months. They also have billiards.

Children's Activities

There are many summertime programs available for children; there are short-term entertainment possibilities as well. The island has two day camps: the Felix Neck Wildlife Sanctuary (627–4850) and the St.

Pierre School Day Camp in Vineyard Haven, which has sailing, tennis, crafts, and other activities (693–1878).

The Old Sculpin Art Gallery in Edgartown, the Nathan Mayhew Seminars, and the Vineyard Summer School at the regional high school (693–1033) have art, athletic programs, and other classes for children. The Vineyard Dance, part of the Nathan Mayhew Seminars' summer program, has classes in ballet and modern dance, as well as the Island Theatre Workshop Children's Theatre (693–4060). Some of the boat rental places give boating, sailing, and sailboarding lessons to children. Many of the tennis courts have instructors to give children lessons, and there are horseback riding classes available. The community center in Chilmark has a full summer program, so if you are staying there, be sure to call (645–9484).

The libraries all have storytelling hours and some have movies, so call about their schedules.

The Flying Horses carousel in Oak Bluffs is a great favorite with children. It is open from 1:00 to 9:00 P.M. daily, spring through fall.

Children will probably enjoy the museums on the island. The Vineyard Museum will interest children over 8 years old. They also will

An intrepid rider reaches for the brass ring at Oak Bluffs' famous Flying Horses, one of the oldest carousels in the country.

enjoy watching the presses run at the *Vineyard Gazette* office in Edgartown or touring the state lobster hatchery. Outdoor lovers will appreciate the wildlife preserves and visiting Takemmy Farm in North Tisbury to see the llamas and miniature donkeys. It is open two afternoons a week; it's best to call, 693–1828.

Finally, the public schools in all the towns have athletic fields where visitors can play ball, and there are swings, slides, and basketball courts as well. Vineyard Haven also has an athletic field behind the post office.

Concerts

There are many concerts and musical programs all summer long at the Tabernacle, the Chilmark Community Center, the Old Whaling Church, and various other locations. It's advisable to check the schedules in the newspaper each week. Arlo Guthrie, Dave Brubeck, Harry Connick, Jr., James Taylor, Carly Simon, and others have performed on the Vineyard in past summers.

Evening Entertainment

The Hot Tin Roof at Martha's Vineyard Airport and The Atlantic Connection are the two nightclubs on the island. Started by Carly Simon and others, The Hot Tin Roof has been very popular and features many nationally known entertainers. Consult your paper for announcements.

There are places with piano bars and singers, including The Seafood Shanty and The Wharf in Edgartown; Anthony's, David's Island House, and The Atlantic Connection in Oak Bluffs; and the very popular Wintertide in Vineyard Haven, a nonprofit establishment that is open year-round and features amateur and professional entertainers.

Fall Foliage

Unlike the wildflowers, which should never be picked, gathering dried grasses in the fall won't hurt the plants. The salt hay, oats, and other marsh grasses, milkweed pods, cattails, and bittersweet (which grows everywhere and is destructive but pretty) make very attractive arrangements.

Fishing

The tricky tides swirling around the island will largely determine an angler's luck. As many as three different tides are said to converge at Edgartown Harbor. High tide at Gay Head can vary as much as an hour from that inside Menemsha Pond. High tide at Cape Pogue on Chappaquiddick is eight hours different from that at Gay Head, and the tide difference between Edgartown and Vineyard Haven is thirty minutes. The *Vineyard Gazette* prints a tide chart each week, and the Eldridge *Tide Book* is helpful in determining when to fish where. Some of the best shore fishing spots on the island also are some of the most popular. Both bluefish and bonito are caught along the Chappaquiddick shore at Cape Pogue and Wasque and at Lobsterville Beach in Gay Head. Some anglers have luck at the stone jetties at State Beach between Oak Bluffs and Edgartown and at the entrance to Menemsha Harbor. Scup is found in the inner and outer harbors everywhere, while the once plentiful flounder, which prefer the sandy shoals, have become scarce. Don't be concerned if you're a novice and bring in what's locally known as a sand shark; they are harmless and quite common. Cod, which are caught in the cool weather during spring and fall, are not ordinarily considered a game fish, but they have become increasingly popular with sport fishers.

Fishing Offshore

Chartering a boat to go trolling offshore for blues, bluefin tuna, shark, and white marlin is very popular. In Edgartown there are six charter boats, and it is best to check with the harbormaster at 627–4746, or Larry's Tackle Shop at 627–5088. In Oak Bluffs call the harbormaster, 693–4355, where two charter boats are available, in Vineyard Haven call 693–7792, and in Menemsha check with the harbormaster at 645–2846. Consult the paper for information about other sailboats and motorboats available for short sight-seeing trips or longer cruises.

Flight Instruction

Flying lessons are available at Martha's Vineyard Airport. It is best to go and inquire, as the availability of instructors varies from year to year.

The Vineyard's stone jetties are popular spots with anglers.

Golf

There are two public golf courses on the island, and they are both Down-Island. Farm Neck Golf Links, which overlooks Sengekontacket Pond and the state beach, is located off County Road in Oak Bluffs. An eighteen-hole championship course, Farm Neck has a driving range, fully equipped pro shop with rental equipment, and buckets of balls for the driving range. For further information call 693–3057. The Mink Meadows Golf Club is an eighteen-hole course in West Chop just off Franklin Street. Call 693–0600.

On State Road in Vineyard Haven, there's an eighteen-hole miniature golf course (Island Cove Miniature Golf Course, 693–2611) that is tastefully landscaped with waterfalls and planting. Open spring to fall, there is handicapped access for the first nine holes.

A game of golf is a good way to appreciate the island's beautiful scenery.

Horseback Riding

Riding has become increasingly popular on the island; many local children have their own horses, and families summering here for a good part of the season sometimes bring horses with them. Scrubby Neck Stables in West Tisbury, along the south shore opposite the airport, is quite large. They operate year-round and offer both children's and adults' classes. For further information call 693–3770. Pond View Farm on New Lane in West Tisbury (693–2949), Misty Meadows Horse Farm on the Old County Road (693–1870), and Iron Hill Riding Stables (693–0786) also offer trail rides, lessons, and boarding facilities.

Island Tours

The best way to become acquainted with the island is to take walking tours of the three Down-Island towns and a driving tour of the rest of the island, as described in the last four chapters of this book. There also are guided tours in buses and taxi-vans that originate at the ferry landings.

Lectures

Lectures on the island are too numerous to list individually. All the churches, performing arts centers, and other public gathering places seem to have their share of lectures each summer. Because there are so many summer visitors in the art, academic, television, and business worlds who volunteer their services for one group or another, the lecture choices are quite unusual. It's best to check your newspaper each week for the upcoming events.

Libraries

Each of the six towns has its own public library. They all have children's reading and storytelling programs. Summer visitors may get library cards, even if they're only staying briefly on the island, and the cards are good for one year.

In Edgartown there is no charge for a library card if you are a Massachusetts resident; otherwise it is $5. The library is on North Water Street.

In Oak Bluffs there is a $3 charge for visitors and non-property own-ers who wish to get a library card. There is no charge for a property owner. The library is on Circuit Avenue.

In Vineyard Haven there is a charge of $5 for visitors and non-property owners to get a library card. The library is on Main Street.

In West Tisbury and Gay Head anyone may get a library card and there is no charge for it. The libraries are in the center of town. In Chilmark there is no charge for a library card, and anyone who is stay-ing in town may get one.

Museums

The island has three interesting museums to visit. They are the Vine-yard Museum in Edgartown, the tiny Old Schoolhouse Museum with artifacts that date back to the Revolution in Vineyard Haven, and the Cottage Museum in Oak Bluffs on the Camp Ground.

The Vineyard Museum

On School and Cooke Streets in Edgartown is the interesting complex of buildings that make up the Vineyard Museum. The twelve rooms of the Thomas Cooke House are furnished with early island artifacts, in-cluding costumes, dolls, a large collection of whaling material, and more.

The main building houses the Gale Huntington Library of History and the Francis Foster Museum. The library is the island's major his-torical library and repository of documents, log books, charts used by the Royal Navy during the Revolutionary War, genealogical materials, plus thousands of old books about the history of Martha's Vineyard. The Francis Foster Museum houses scrimshaw, whaling material, ship models, maritime paintings, products of early local industries, and a display of Nancy Luce's poetry and tombstones for her pet chickens.

There is a boat shed containing a whaleboat, a peddler's wagon, a Button hand-pump fire engine used from 1854 to 1925 (and in the is-land's Fourth of July parade), a Noman's Land boat, beautifully woven Indian eel pots, and many other items. Also on the Society's property is the old Fresnel lens from the early Gay Head Lighthouse. The adjacent building on School Street was recently bought for additional space, and contributions to this project are welcome.

The museum's buildings are open daily from 10:00 A.M. to 4:30 P.M. Admission charges are as follows: adults are $2 in the winter and $4 in

the summer; children under 12 are free year-round; children 12 to 18 years are $1 in the winter and $2 in the summer; senior citizens are $1 in the winter and $2 in the summer. The museum's telephone number is 627–4441.

The Old School House Museum

Formerly called the DAR Museum and originally a school, this museum on Main Street in Vineyard Haven is now owned by the Martha's Vineyard Preservation Trust. It's tiny, with an interesting display of island artifacts from the whaling era and the eighteenth century. Call 627–8017 for visiting hours.

Cottage Museum

An antique-filled gingerbread house on the campground at Trinity Park in Oak Bluffs will delight anyone interested in the interiors of these tiny Carpenter Gothic houses. Open Monday through Saturday during the summer.

Nature Walks

Nature walks have become increasingly popular in recent years. Because of the migratory flight path over the island and the mild climate, the variety and abundance of flora and birds are unusual. All the wildlife sanctuaries are open for hiking through the woods and alongshore; some also allow picnicking and swimming. Different conservation groups sponsor nature walks, and it's best to check the local paper or call Felix Neck (627–4850) or the Vineyard Conservation Society (693–9588) for information.

If you're here for a short visit and would like to see four very different areas, the wooded Cedar Tree Neck along the north shore, the flat plains of the mid-island state forest, Chappaquiddick's outer rim at the Wasque preserve, and Lobsterville's Cranberry Lands will show you the island's enormous natural diversity.

Shell Collecting

The desire to pick up a pretty shell on the beach is irresistible to most people. The shells on the island aren't outstanding, but there are some attractive ones, particularly the scallop shells, which are found near the drawbridge in Vineyard Haven, the Oak Bluffs end of the state beach near the bridge and jetties, around the Edgartown Lighthouse, and on Lobsterville Beach. There are almost no shells on the south shore.

Shellfishing

If you enjoy the island, the best thing you can do for those who live here is not to go shellfishing at all. It is an important part of the local economy for residents, and the inexperienced or careless visitor can damage the clam beds and kill the baby scallops very easily. There is a great effort now underway to increase the growth and development of clams, oysters, lobsters, and scallops. Abuse of shellfish beds is against the law.

Shopping

There are many gift shops, clothing stores, handcraft shops, and art galleries, as well as T-shirt shops and souvenir stores. There are some very attractive shops with hand-knit sweaters, sport clothes, unusual gifts, and antique and locally made gold jewelry. Many shops carry the work of local craftspeople, from furniture, clothes, quilts, and pottery to lovely weathervanes, and all of the shops are busy on rainy days.

Tennis

All the towns but Gay Head now have tennis courts for the public. In Edgartown there are town courts located behind the Edgartown Fire Department on Robinson Road (no telephone), and at the Martha's Vineyard Regional High School on the Edgartown–Vineyard Haven Road. The private courts on the Katama Road are rented out to the public. In Oak Bluffs the courts at the Island Inn are open to the public (693–6574). There are town courts available on Tuckernuck Avenue (no telephone), as well as at Farm Neck located on the County Road (693–9728). There are two town courts in the center of Vineyard Haven on Church Street, and they have a free clinic for children under 15. At the grammar school in West Tisbury on Old County Road there are courts available. Reservations must be made a day in advance, but there is no telephone. The Chilmark Community Center at Beetlebung Corner has tennis for Chilmark residents and summer visitors staying in the town. Call 645–3061 for information.

Theater

There are three movie theaters in the Down-Island towns, which feature the latest films all summer long. In Oak Bluffs there are two seasonal theaters at the busy intersection at the foot of Circuit Avenue, and in Vineyard Haven the theater on Main Street is open all year. For information call 627–7469.

At the Vineyard Playhouse, located on Church Street in Vineyard Haven, a professional New York theater group and amateurs stage plays and musicals in season (693–6450). The Island Theatre is a year-round workshop for adults and children. The Yard, a professional dance group from New York, has its own attractive theater in a renovated barn at Beetlebung Corner in Chilmark. The performers, choreographers, composers, and directors live and work within the complex throughout the summer season. Call 645–9662 for details on productions.

Tours and Interesting Places to Visit

The island is full of many interesting places to visit, most of which are included in the museum section of this chapter or in the island tours. In addition, you may enjoy knowing about the following:

Vineyard Gazette

The *Vineyard Gazette* office on South Summer Street at the corner of Davis Lane in Edgartown is an interesting place to visit. There is a glass-enclosed room on the side of the building where visitors can watch the newspaper presses running.

Vincent House

The Vincent House on Main Street in Edgartown is owned by the Martha's Vineyard Preservation Trust and is open to the public to demonstrate how houses of the seventeenth century were constructed. Its hours during the summer are 10:00 A.M. to noon Monday through Friday.

Flying Horses Carousel

This Oak Bluffs carousel, one of the oldest in the nation, is a must-see for island visitors. The handsome wooden horses are more than a century old, and the carousel has been listed on the National Register of Historic Places. It is open 1:00 to 9:00 P.M. daily, from spring through fall.

Chicama Vineyards

On State Road outside of Vineyard Haven are the Chicama Vineyards. Chicama produces several different kinds of wines from a variety of European grapes. It is the first winery ever licensed in Massachusetts, and visitors may tour the vineyard and the winery. Grapevine wreaths, wine, and gift items are offered for sale. Tours are held from 11:00 A.M. to 5:00 P.M. Monday through Saturday.

Shakespeare Garden

Behind the library in Vineyard Haven is the Shakespeare Garden. It was created in memory of Margaret Webster, the renowned Shakespearean scholar who summered on the Vineyard.

State Lobster Hatchery

In Vineyard Haven on Shirley Avenue, off County Road, is the state lobster hatchery. Here, in a laboratory with its tanks and marine biology equipment, valuable research and experiments are being done on the living habits of lobsters. The hatchery is nationally known in the scientific community for its accomplishments in expediting the growth process of lobsters, and there is an attendant on duty to explain the work being done here. The hatchery is open daily, year-round, and there is no admission charge.

Wildlife Sanctuaries

The island's wildlife areas are open to the public year-round. They are open, natural areas of woods, beach, marsh, and pond. These sanctuaries are primarily for walking in and enjoying nature in its undisturbed state. The untiring efforts and financial contributions of many people have made these areas available to the public and kept them from being developed, ensuring that future generations will have the opportunity to enjoy a pristine environment. Approximately 20 percent of the island's total land mass in now protected.

There are specially guided nature and bird walks, often to raise

Wild turkeys roam the fields and woodlands Up-Island.

money for a given sanctuary; these are announced in the paper. There is no admission charge to these wildlife sanctuaries, and no swimming or picnicking is allowed except where noted below. All of the sanctuaries listed below are easily accessible. There are still others, if you are interested; information on them can be obtained at the Vineyard Conservation Society Office at the Wakeman Conservation Center on Lambert's Cove Road.

Edgartown

The Felix Neck Wildlife Sanctuary is located off the Edgartown–Vineyard Haven Road. This is a unique, 350-acre wildlife preserve of beach, marsh, open fields, and woodland. It is run by the Massachusetts Audubon Society. It offers the summer visitor a network of 6 miles of marked nature trails with a photography blind and an observation blind to watch waterfowl on Sengekontacket Pond. In the barn there are nature displays, a library, and booklets for sale. They also run a summer day camp.

Mashackett Neck is a 75-acre preserve owned by the town of Edgartown as a wildlife preserve. It borders Edgartown Great Pond and is located off Meetinghouse Way.

Sheriff's Meadow is a 16-acre preserve off Planting Field Way. There are foot trails around Sheriff's Meadow Pond through woods, marshland, and along a path that affords a lovely view of Eel Pond and Nantucket Sound.

Wasque Reservation is a 200-acre preserve of dune and beach bordering Katama Bay on the southeast corner of Chappaquiddick. Swimming, picnicking, and fishing are permitted.

Vineyard Haven

West Chop Woods, off Franklin Street, is an 83-acre preserve owned by the Sheriff's Meadow Foundation. There are marked trails but no facilities of any kind here.

North Tisbury

Cedar Tree Neck is a 250-acre preserve on the north shore that is operated by the Sheriff's Meadow Foundation. From State Road in North Tisbury heading toward Vineyard Haven, take Indian Hill Road to the sanctuary. There are color-coded, marked trails through the woods and along the beach. It is a fine place for nature study and hiking.

West Tisbury

Martha's Vineyard State Forest, practically in the center of the island, is a 4,000-acre preserve in West Tisbury and Edgartown. A marked nature trail begins at the headquarters off Airport Road. There are 14 miles of paved bike paths and fire lanes for horseback riding.

Chilmark

Menemsha Hills Reservation is a 200-acre preserve operated by the Trustees of Reservations. Located off the North Road, midway between Tabor House Road and Menemsha Cross Road, there is a parking area. There are marked foot trails leading down to the rocky shore, and swimming and fishing are permitted.

Middle Road Sanctuary, off Middle Road in Chilmark, is owned by the Sheriff's Meadow Foundation. There are no marked trails, but it's a fine spot for nature study.

Peaked Hill is a small lookout and one of the highest points on the island. It is approximately a half-mile up Middle Road from Beetlebung Corner. Park on Middle Road and walk up.

Skiing the dunes along the south shore.

The island's ponds provide good ice skating in the middle of winter.

Cedar Tree Neck Wildlife Sanctuary

Retrace your steps to the hard-surfaced road. A right turn on Indian Hill Road goes to the Cedar Tree Neck Wildlife Sanctuary. There are several old Cape houses in this rural setting that are unspoiled by development; they show what these self-sufficient island communities looked like a hundred years ago.

The road climbs to a sharp curve where a sign points the way down a very narrow, bumpy dirt road for a mile to the 250-acre wildlife sanctuary. It is maintained as a "natural habitat for wildlife and as a living museum for the enjoyment of all who love the outdoors and wish to follow the marked trails through the woods and along the beach and to look out from the height of Cedar Tree Neck." With its herring pond, meadows, rocky bluffs, woodland of scrub oak and beech trees, bayberry, and freshwater stream flowing into the sea, this unusually varied terrain exemplifies the character of the island's north shore.

The popular Book Den East in Oak Bluffs sells used and rare books.

From the high neck of land here, one can visualize how the shoreline must have looked a century ago when the Sound was white with sails from workboats, and fish traps were strung out from shore to catch the mackerel, butterfish, squiteaque, and other schools of fish moving through Vineyard Sound.

Winter Sports

Winter sports on the island can be a great deal of fun. When there's snow on the ground, cross-country skiers hurry out to the beaches to ski. There is an ice-skating rink in Oak Bluffs on the inland road between Edgartown and Vineyard Haven. Skating lessons, hockey games, and public skating are offered. Telephone the ice arena at 693–4438 for more information. Ice skating is enjoyed on ponds whenever the weather is especially cold.

Tisbury Health Club on Main Street in Vineyard Haven has an indoor swimming pool and exercise classes. Call 693–2200. There are many other exercise classes available.

Winter or Summer Reading

Bookstores on the island stock the best hardcover books and popular paperbacks for the beach. The Bunch of Grapes in Vineyard Haven, the island's premier bookstore, is very large and exceptionally well stocked. The popular Book Den East in Oak Bluffs has a barn full of wonderful used and rare books. In the center of Edgartown, the Bickerton and Ripley Bookstore is small but has a fine selection for rainy-day browsing. The Fligors of Edgartown, a large gift, clothing, and toy store, has carried books about the island and volumes by island authors for years. They also have a splendid array of children's books. Also check the charming gift shop, The Secret Garden, in Oak Bluffs.

There are many nationally and internationally known writers summering or living most of the year on the Vineyard, and the stores give autograph parties for their latest work. It's best to check the newspaper notices for them. Because of the large number of authors, Bunch of Grapes has weekly book-signing parties all summer long.

10

ANNUAL SPECIAL EVENTS

April

Easter Morning Service

There is a sunrise service held on Easter morning at the Gay Head Cliffs. The Aquinnah Shop opens for the season and serves an early morning breakfast.

May

Memorial Day

The island's annual Memorial Day parade is held in Edgartown, Oak Bluffs, or Vineyard Haven. Edgartown always has a special ceremony, whether or not it has the parade, and children toss their bouquets from the town wharf into the harbor in memory of all the Vineyarders who have died at sea.

Dinner Dance

A dinner dance is held the last weekend of May at the Harborview Hotel in Edgartown to benefit the Martha's Vineyard Preservation Trust.

June

A recent, extremely popular event is the farmer's market held on Saturdays in the center of West Tisbury. Fresh garden vegetables, baked goods, crafts, flowers, and other items draw a large crowd from June through September.

July

Fourth of July Parade

The Fourth of July parade in Edgartown is a tradition. The small but colorful event includes the Button hand-pump fire engine from the Vineyard Museum, children from the cerebral palsy camp, floats, bagpipers, antique cars, and other participants.

Tisbury Street Fair

A few days after Independence Day is the Tisbury Street Fair in Vineyard Haven. This has become a large event. Main Street is closed for the day, and artists, craftspeople, merchants, farmers, bakers, and delicatessen owners line the thoroughfare to sell their wares.

Edgartown Regatta

Many yacht clubs along the Massachusetts coast enter the Edgartown Regatta, held in mid-July. The largest sailing event in the area, there are nine or ten one-design classes of smaller boats, and six classes in two divisions of the larger cruising boats.

Also in mid-July, every other summer the New York Yacht Club usually has a one-day rendezvous in Edgartown. The harbor is colorful and crowded; many large vessels are in full dress, with signal flags running from bow to stern.

The Edgartown Regatta in mid-July is the area's largest sailing event.

Annual Craft Fair

Sponsored by Vineyard craftspeople, the annual craft fair in mid-July is a large, four-day event held at the island's high school on the Edgartown–Vineyard Haven Road. Handcrafts, art, sculpture, and other items made by local and off-island craftspeople are for sale in the various booths. Proceeds go to the school's athletic and music programs.

Celebrity Tennis and Croquet Tournaments

To raise money for the Nathan Mayhew Seminars, both tennis and croquet tournaments take place on the same weekend in mid-July.

Mike and Mary Wallace, Walter Cronkite, Art Buchwald, Rose Styron (author William Styron's wife), Beverly Sills, and others give generously of their time for the cause. Some play in both tournaments. The tennis matches are held in one of the three Down-Island towns. For the croquet matches, which are held at the Harborview Hotel, the women dress in Victorian fashions.

Annual Portuguese Celebration and Feast

Every year in late July there is a Portuguese Celebration and Feast at the Portuguese-American Club grounds on Vineyard Avenue in Oak Bluffs. The weekend event includes an auction, lots of Portuguese food, dancing, and a Sunday parade to the club, where free soup is served. The Portuguese came to Martha's Vineyard very early when they served aboard whaling and merchant ships, and there is a large population on the island today who are proud of their heritage.

Oak Bluffs House Tour

The Cottagers, a women's club in Oak Bluffs, has an annual house tour to raise money for several organizations. There are six houses on the tour each summer; the last house always serves tea, and the tours have been very popular.

August

Possible Dreams Auction

This has become the most hilarious and popular charity event during the summer. In a ten-gallon hat, chomping a cigar, auctioneer Art

Buchwald sounds forth with his rapid-fire wit. He has even carried on in a sudden squall.

The auction, which benefits Martha's Vineyard Community Services, takes place in early August by the swimming pool at the Harborside Inn in Edgartown. Buchwald puts up for bid all sorts of unusual and fascinating items: a sail with Walter Cronkite; a picnic with author William Styron; a tour of CBS Studios with Mike Wallace; a tour of the *Washington Post* with publisher Katherine Graham; and other original prizes. It draws a large crowd, so it's best to come early and advisable to bring your own chair. The admission is $15.

All Island Art Show

This art show takes place in early August at the Tabernacle in Oak Bluffs. Anyone may submit entries for consideration by the three judges. Details are available at the Camp Ground Meeting Association, 693–0525.

Edgartown House Tour

Held the first Tuesday of August every year, this house tour is very popular. The majority of the five houses on the tour are historic buildings. Tea is served in a sixth house. Each year the houses chosen are either on the south or the north side of town, all within easy walking distance of one another. The proceeds are for the hospital.

Crafts and Collectibles Show

This show, also sponsored by the Camp Ground Meeting Association, takes place in early or mid-August at the Tabernacle. For more information call 693–0525.

Annual Fireworks Display

In mid-August the Oak Bluffs Fire Department puts on a fireworks display at State Beach, which is on the road to Edgartown. It gets very crowded, so come early.

Antiques Show

The Edgartown Public Library holds an antiques show in the middle of August at the Edgartown Grammar School. Antique dealers from Con-

Weighing in a catch
during the fall Striped
Bass and Bluefish Derby
in Vineyard Haven.
(right)

The annual fireworks
display in Oak Bluffs
is a very popular mid-
August event. The
gazebo in Ocean Park,
where concerts are held
all summer, is in the
foreground. (far right)

Summertime visitors
study the art exhibited
at the All Island Art
Show in Oak Bluffs.
(below)

necticut, New York, and other areas rent space for this annual three-day event. For more information call 627–4421.

Illumination Night

During this century-old tradition in Oak Bluffs, each gingerbread house in the Camp Ground area is hung with a myriad of Japanese lanterns, creating a fairyland of twinkling lights. The tradition originated to signify the closing of the Camp Ground for another season. It takes place in mid-August.

Martha's Vineyard Agricultural Society Fair and Livestock Show

The livestock show and fair has been held for well over a century in West Tisbury. It takes place at the fairgrounds and Agricultural Hall.

It has become a major three-day event in mid-August and has all the country fair attractions: horse show, cattle, sheep, oxen, fruits, vegetables, baked goods, balloons, games of chance, wood-chopping contests, a ferris wheel, and more.

A team getting ready for the horse-drawing contest, one of the oldest and most popular events at the Martha's Vineyard Agricultural Society Fair and Livestock Show in West Tisbury.

For over a century, the popular Martha's Vineyard Agricultural Society Fair and Livestock Show has been held in West Tisbury. Originally, exhibits of farm produce and baked goods, along with woodsmen and horse-drawing contests, were the featured events, but now the fair also has many carnival attractions.

Chilmark Road Race

This road race has become extremely popular. It's a series of 3-mile races for different age groups and is open to amateurs. It is held in late August, and an entry fee is charged. Consult the paper for announcements.

September

Tivoli Day

On Tivoli Day, a Saturday in the middle of September, bicycle races are held in Oak Bluffs. The event has become part of the United States Cycling Federation National Prestige Classic circuit. There is the round-the-island race, as well as shorter races for all ages and talents around the course at Ocean Park. Other festivities are held, including a street fair on Circuit Avenue. The name of the day originated in the 1870s,

Tivoli Day Bike Races in Oak Bluffs.

when a large dance hall called the Tivoli ("I lov it" spelled backward) was built next to the carousel. The name also was used for a roller-skating rink and a song title.

Striped Bass and Bluefish Derby

For more than forty years, the Striped Bass and Bluefish Derby has been held from mid-September to mid-October. As many as 2,000 anglers sign up to try their skills in landing striped bass, bluefish, bonito, false albacore, and weakfish from boat and shore. Prizes are given daily

and weekly, and finally there are grand prizes. For information and entry blanks, contact the Chamber of Commerce in Vineyard Haven, 693–0085.

November

Ducks Unlimited Dinner

Ducks Unlimited is a national organization concerned with the welfare of waterfowl. The local chapter holds this dinner in late fall at the Har-

Scallop shell ornaments are hung on trees in Edgartown's mini-park each December.

borview Hotel in Edgartown to raise money for its various conservation programs.

December

Christmas in Edgartown

Christmas festivities are held in Edgartown for three days on the second weekend of December. Many inns offer special rates for the weekend. There are walking tours, horse-and-buggy rides around town, musical programs at the Old Whaling Church, and a parade; sherry, eggnog, tea, and mulled wines are offered to shoppers in various stores. Santa arrives at the mini-park in downtown Edgartown, where children gather around the Christmas tree they've decorated with painted scallop shells. The Vineyard Museum has a special Christmas exhibition. There's a special island-made handicrafts sale, and a buffet dinner-dance is held at the Harborview Hotel to benefit the Edgartown Boys' and Girls' Club.

Vineyard Haven also has a special Christmas celebration called "The Twelve Days of Christmas," which takes place in mid-month.

11

ISLAND ARCHITECTURE

The history of Martha's Vineyard is reflected in its houses, both the interiors and the exteriors. There are seven different styles spanning three centuries. The periods overlap, just as they did on the mainland, but with the islanders' natural reluctance to change, the time spans were often longer and exact dates somewhat obscure. None of the original settlers' houses remain, but the earliest houses were Cape style and were built without the benefit of an architect. Most of them have been extensively remodeled, but the Vincent House in Edgartown has not. It is a prime example of an early Cape, and, fortunately, it is open to the public.

There are full, half, and three-quarter Capes. The full Cape has a large central chimney supporting several fireplaces and a symmetrical window placement, with two windows on either side of the front door. The windows have small, square panes, usually twelve-over-twelve. Based on a style from Devon and Cornwall in England, the one-story Cape, held down against the wind by its snug gable roof (whose eaves come down to touch the front door and windows), hugs the ground, and generally faces south. The steep shed roof serves as both roof and wall, the ceilings are low, and the tiny, narrow stairs are just inside the entryway, set against the chimney.

There are half Capes with the front door at one end of the house, two windows, and the chimney usually directly above the front door. The three-quarter Cape is also asymmetrical, with two windows on one side of the front door, one window on the other, and an off-center chimney.

The attic room in the Cape was used for sleeping as well as for storing onions, cranberries, smoked herring, and other food that could hang from rafters. A small cellar, often called a root cellar, served as a refrigerator. It was usually a round, brick enclosure resembling a large well, where vegetables, apples, beer, milk, and other foods were kept cold.

As time went on and more materials became available, two-and-a-half-story Capes were built. By the first quarter of the nineteenth century, most of these houses had added a kitchen ell across the rear of the house, which was called a porch by islanders. This addition was very common throughout the Massachusetts Bay Colony. Often a small room in the ell was used for a creamery. With this ell—or lean-to—across the rear of the house, it had a saltbox profile. This design became very common in New England, but there are almost no true saltboxes on the island.

Houses built in the elegant Georgian style (1720–1780) do not exist on the island. The wealth came later during the whaling era. Instead, in this period the Vineyard produced foursquare Colonial houses with

The Vincent House in Edgartown, built in the seventeenth century, is a prime example of an early Cape. (top)

There are very few saltbox houses on the Vineyard. This one is in West Tisbury. (bottom)

modest adaptations of the Georgian style. They were often built by ships' carpenters with the help of books from England. Two separated chimneys provide a central hall plan with a wide staircase, closets by the chimneys, moldings, a paneled fireplace wall, and a kitchen ell with another chimney to accommodate an iron cookstove. The paneled front door has a row of windows at the top to let in light. On the eve of the Revolution, rectangular and elliptical fanlights over the door became popular, as did sidelights, and they were often made of colored

Greek Revival architecture was popular on the island in the mid-nineteenth century. (top)

The Wooden Valentine in Oak Bluffs was built during the Victorian period. (bottom)

The Captain's House in Edgartown is a good example of Federal and Greek Revival Architecture. (left)

glass. Cranberry glass was the most popular; it allowed the light in while the owner could peek out without being seen. The squared-off pillars on either side of the door are set flat against the building and the double-hung sash windows have twelve-over-twelve windowpanes.

The brief, post-Revolutionary Federal period (1776–1840) was a time of great prosperity and burgeoning architecture on the island. The newborn nation's carpenters and shipwrights, with the help of architects in many cases, adopted the warm, delicate detail of the Federal style, which architectural historians have called one of America's "greatest architectural achievements." These large, square, five-bay houses show a mastery of composition, restraint, and grace of detail in the balusters around the hip roof. They usually have elliptical arched fanlights and sidelights, a small projecting portico, spiral staircases, and beautifully carved mantels and moldings. Even the fences, enclosing yards of clipped boxwood and yew (instead of sprawling lilacs and roses), are masterpieces of craftwork. Modest adornments from the Federal period are found on Edgartown houses built at this time. Many island houses are transitional, with up-and-coming Greek Revival pillars adorning the portico and the delicately carved roof rails, such as those on the Daniel Fisher house.

By 1840, Greek Revival architecture had swept up the coast from Jefferson's Virginia. This style was best suited to public buildings; however, the classical doorways with pillars and the cool aestheticism of the style appealed to New Englanders, and they adopted it. Edgartown's Methodist Church is the island's outstanding example. To imitate the white limestone of Greek temples, these buildings were painted white, and the tradition has carried on for all the houses.

As the initial fervor for these Greek adaptations subsided, a new era in architecture, named for Queen Victoria, began to appear. The Victorian era was known for its prudishness; this exterior pretense, as evidenced by lace, frills, and skirts on furniture, also found its way into the charming lacy architecture of the period with the invention of the jigsaw and fretsaw used for scrollwork.

It was an era that the American poet Amy Lowell called "that long set of sentimental hypocrisies known in England as Victoria"; nonetheless, it did produce the fascinating architecture that can be seen in Oak Bluffs. Tents in the Camp Ground were hastily converted into little wooden houses, each with four rooms (a living room and bedroom downstairs and two bedrooms upstairs; the cooking was done in cook tents, and there was no plumbing). All had front porches facing the Tabernacle in the center of the lawn. The lacy, wedding-cake patterns of Carpenter Gothic, with shingles like pigeon feathers, decorated

The Menemsha boat house is part of the history of island architecture.

every "wooden tent" on the Camp Ground, making it a landmark in gingerbread architecture. A few other Victorian buildings can be found in the other towns.

The other structures that have a unique place in the history of island architecture are the fishermen's boat houses. Without them, the town of Menemsha, which relates so strongly to the sea, would lose its character and its visual history. These simple, practical workshops are made from white-cedar shingles weathered a silvery gray in the salt air. The lobster pots piled high outside, and the rope blocks, lobster buoys, carpentry tools, potbellied stove, and all manner of gear cluttering the interior are the link between the fisherman and his vessel tied up alongside Dutcher's Dock. The fishermen's gray-weathered homes up above the bluff and the fishing fleet give the coastal village its unique character.

12

VINEYARD HAVEN TOUR

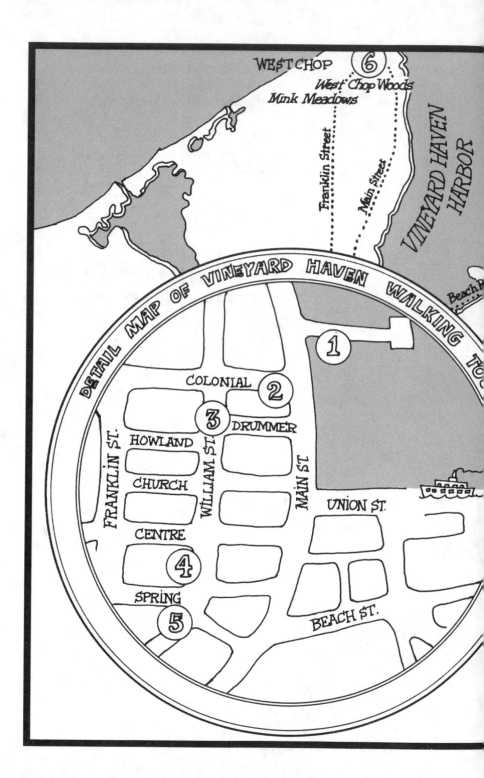

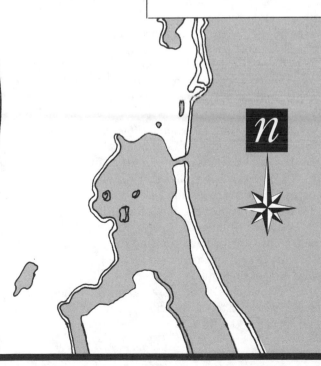

EAST CHOP

Highland Rd.

⑦

Crystal Lake

• EASTVILLE

Vineyard Haven

Points of Interest

1. OWEN PARK
2. LIBERTY POLE MUSEUM
3. WILLIAM STREET
4. ASSOCIATION HALL
5. CAPTAIN RICHARD C. LUCE HOUSE
6. WEST CHOP
7. EAST CHOP

n

Because Vineyard Haven is the island's commercial center and principal port of entry, we'll begin our first tour here and encircle the island in a clockwise direction.

The first white settlement here began in 1674, thirty-two years after Edgartown, and was known as Holmes Hole for two centuries. In Colonial times it was customary to call a protected anchorage a "hole," while the surname attached to it was usually the first person to use it or the owner of the adjoining land.

Holmes Hole was a village within the township of Tisbury. In 1671 when Tisbury received its charter, it was a farming community, and the center of town was the present Up-Island village of West Tisbury. As the little port of Holmes Hole began to grow with the movement of maritime traffic through Vineyard Sound, it separated from West Tisbury, established its own post office, and changed its name to Vineyard Haven in 1871. The town later was legally named Tisbury, however, which is confusing to the newcomer who will see both names used, although Vineyard Haven is more common.

The growth of Vineyard Haven as an important seaport along the East Coast began with the expansion of trade with the West Indies and coastal shipping. It became a refuge for coastwise traffic, and in the nineteenth century as many as 200 vessels at a time would be in the harbor to replenish supplies, ride out a storm, or wait for a favoring tide and wind. Shipyards, sail lofts, coopers, bakers, blacksmiths, and general stores sprang up along the waterfront to provision the coastal schooners, deepwater vessels, sloops, packets, colliers, and tugs that put into the harbor. Even the men and women who were farmers profited when their "bumboats," which were floating peddler's carts, went out to meet the incoming vessels to sell everything from butter and fresh vegetables to hand-knitted socks.

Neither war nor fire has spared Vineyard Haven in its 300 years. During the American Revolution, when the British Commonwealth could no longer spare troops for the island's defense, Vineyarders maintained an uneasy neutrality. In 1778, however, Major General Gray sailed into the harbor with a large force of British troops and eighty-three vessels to replenish supplies. He called together the town authorities, explained his mission, and threatened to burn the town if they resisted. For five days the Vineyard militia was ordered to bring in 300 cattle and thousands of sheep, turn over their arms, and give up public money that belonged to the King of England.

During the War of 1812, Vineyarders again were harassed by the British. Yankee ingenuity was sorely tested in the effort to get supplies through by outwitting and outsailing the British.

On August 11, 1883, tragedy struck the port when a fire, which started in Crocker's Harness Shop (the present site of the Martha's Vineyard National Bank), swept through the center of town and burned sixty buildings on both sides of Main Street. Fifteen years later, in November 1898, a devastating northeaster hit the coast, and fifty vessels in Vineyard Haven Harbor were either driven ashore or sunk at their moorings in what became known as the Portland Gale.

With the opening of the Cape Cod Canal in 1914 and the increased movement of freight along the coast by trains, trucks, and steamships, Vineyard Haven lost most of its maritime commerce. Shipping was slowly replaced by the resort business and the fishing industry, until today the harbor is crowded with pleasure boats of every description as well as a small fishing fleet.

The following walking tour is a pleasant way to see the town.

1. Owen Park
Main Street

From the ferry, walk up Union Street to Main Street and turn right. A half-block along on the right is the old stone bank, once Crocker's Harness Shop, where the great fire of 1883 started. Continue up the hill, and at the crest the road to your right leads down past the William Barry Owen Park to the beach. There are benches, swings, and a bandstand in the park. Given to the town by Mrs. Owen in memory of her husband, whose father was one of Vineyard Haven's foremost whaling captains, it is the only public beach close to the center of town.

2. Schoolhouse Museum
Main Street and Colonial Lane

Retrace your steps a half-block on Main Street toward town, and the Daughters of the American Revolution (DAR) building on your right, at the corner of Colonial Lane, is the North Schoolhouse. A plaque on the flagpole commemorates "the patriotism of the three girls of this village, Polly Daggett, Parnel Manter and Maria Allen, who destroyed with powder a liberty pole erected near this spot to prevent its capture by the British in 1776. This pole, replacing the other, is erected by the Sea Coast Defense Chapter, D.A.R., 1898."

The building itself was originally the North Schoolhouse, built in 1828, and still has its original bell tower. Historical island artifacts are on display. Open summers Monday through Friday.

3. William Street

Proceed up Colonial Lane 1 block to William Street, the town's handsomest street, which was spared during the great fire of 1883. It is a street of Greek Revival houses, many built by sea captains or others who had profited from the port's prosperity. These formal homes incorporated the latest improvements, such as high ceilings, a parlor heater, a cast-iron kitchen range, and a built-in sink and water pump. The exteriors, embellished with sidelights, fluted columns, and fan-shaped windows, reflected this affluence.

Bear right off Colonial at the corner of William Street for 1 block to the street's end, where you'll see the gray-shingled Grace Episcopal Church. Turn back down William Street. The houses at this end of the street were built a little later than those at the lower end; some have early Victorian details. As you continue down William Street, you will see at the corner of Church Street the large, fieldstone Methodist church that was built in 1922 after an earlier one burned. As you approach Spring Street, you'll see the First Baptist Church on your right.

4. Association Hall
Spring Street

Turn right on Spring Street, and the second building on your right is the Tisbury Town Hall, also called Association Hall. It was built in 1844

A typical nineteenth-century house on historic William Street in Vineyard Haven.

for a Congregational Meetinghouse and was shared by the Baptists at the time. On the second floor is the Katherine Cornell Memorial Theatre, where many plays, concerts, and community activities take place year-round. The theater has handsome murals depicting the island's history, which were done by Stan Murphy, a local artist. Funds to remodel the theater, as well as to restore the grounds and building, were donated by actress Katherine Cornell, who spent a great part of her life on the island.

5. *Captain Richard G. Luce House*
   William Street

Return to William Street and bear right. On your right, tucked away in the middle of the block, is a large, yellow house, built in 1833. It is the most elegant of the William Street homes. Captain Luce made eighteen whaling voyages before he retired, and it was his home that prompted the building of handsome and stately houses along William Street by sea captains who bought property in the area. Return to Main Street.

6. *West Chop*

If you wish to tour the west side of Vineyard Haven Harbor, turn left and head up Main Street past Owen Park to the West Chop Lighthouse, which is 2 miles from town.

The twin headlands of West Chop and East Chop, which cradle Vineyard Haven Harbor, protect this large anchorage from all but a northeast storm. Chop is an old-English term to describe the entrance of a harbor or channel; in the eighteenth century the harbor entrance was called "the neck." West Chop was the site of the first Methodist camp meeting on the Vineyard in 1827.

While the architecture of the various island communities gives them their visual character, when they began to develop as summer colonies in the late nineteenth century, newcomers had a pronounced influence on their social development. West Chop got its start as a summer colony in 1887, when many reserved Bostonians chose this area. It has, through the years, attracted retired military personnel, educators, and businesspeople, as well as well-known actors, journalists, television personalities, and writers. All the island towns produced renowned mariners, and members of the Eldridge family, who once ran a ferry to Woods Hole and still publish the indispensable *Tide Book*, have long been associated with the West Chop area.

As you drive along the bluff, the houses are a mixture of very old buildings (some moved from other parts of the island), large, turn-of-the-century shingled houses, and some contemporary houses. The

The many handsome houses on William Street reflect the affluence of the nineteenth century.

road loops around at the West Chop Lighthouse, first built in 1817, and circles around by the West Chop Tennis Club. A right turn here, onto Franklin Street, leads back to Vineyard Haven. After you make this turn you'll pass the Mink Meadows Public Golf Course and the West Chop woods, a wildlife sanctuary.

At the end of Franklin Street, bear left to return to the center of Vineyard Haven.

7. East Chop

Back in the center of town, at the five corners by the post office, take the Beach Road for Oak Bluffs. You will see a large shipyard and Lagoon Pond on your right. With sufficient warning of a northeaster, many boats go into the Lagoon Pond to wait out the gale just as they did a century or more ago. The lagoon is a good scalloping area, and in the winter months fishing crews can be seen raking the beds from their scallop boats. Also on your right, just before the bridge, there's a ramp for launching small boats.

Just over the bridge is a peninsula of land jutting into Vineyard Haven Harbor that is a public beach and a good area for shell collecting. The small cluster of cottages along the waterfront is called Eastville, and the Martha's Vineyard Hospital is on your right. The original settlement here consisted of a ship's chandler, a one-room school, and several taverns. It was also reputed to be the place where mooncussers plied their trade, and it was known locally as the Barbary Coast. By hanging ships' lanterns on poles and swaying them back and forth to resemble a vessel at anchor, mooncussers lured sailing ships onto the rocks, where their wreckage was fair game for looters.

Keeping to the left and staying alongshore, bear left at the next corner onto Highland Drive. It takes you by Crystal Lake, on your right. Known as Ice House Pond in the days before refrigeration, ice once was cut and stored here. The land around the lake is now a wildlife sanctuary, but it is apt to be too marshy for easy walking.

From the top of the East Chop bluff at the lighthouse, the view across the Sound to Cape Cod is spectacular. The lighthouse marks the eastern entrance to Vineyard Haven Harbor, and was built in 1877 to replace an 1802 signal tower that had burned.

East Chop was called "The Highlands" in the nineteenth century when Baptists started their summer camp meetings here. With Methodists living in what is now the center of Oak Bluffs, the road going by Oak Bluffs Harbor was referred to as "going over Jordan." The architecture in East Chop is a mixture of Carpenter Gothic and the turn-of-the-century shingled cottage. Continuing around a sharp curve at the bottom of the bluff, the East Chop Beach Club and Oak Bluffs Harbor are on your left.

Turn left at the end onto Lake Avenue, which leads to the traffic circle at Oak Bluffs.

A view from the East Chop Lighthouse of the large, shingle-style cottages lining the bluff at East Chop.

13

OAK BLUFFS TOUR

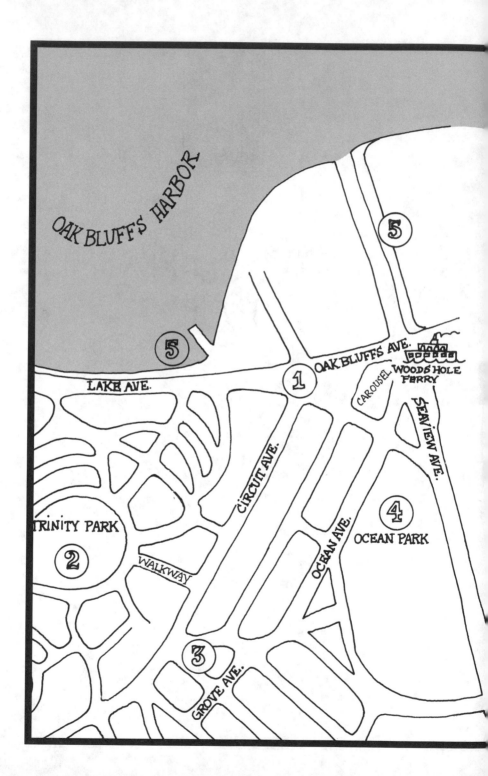

Oak Bluffs

Points of Interest

1. THE FLYING HORSES
2. TRINITY PARK
3. UNION CHAPEL
4. OCEAN PARK
5. BEACH & HARBOR
6. ALONGSHORE TO EDGARTOWN

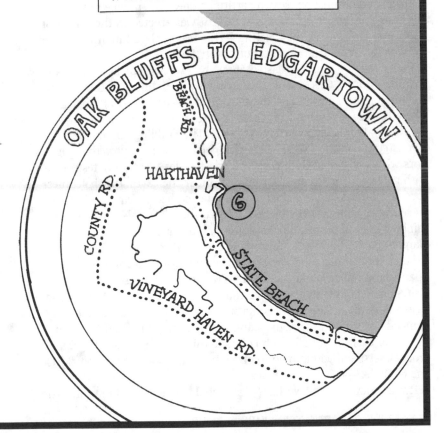

Founded in England in the 1770s by John Wesley, Methodism soon came to America through missionaries; its first appearance on Martha's Vineyard was in 1787 with the arrival of John Saunders, an ex-slave from Virginia. The movement quickly caught fire in America, and in 1827 the first Methodist camp meeting on the island was held in West Chop by "Reformation" John Adams, an itinerant preacher from New Hampshire. The Revivalist service was a public forum for soul searching and emotional displays of doubt and conviction. It was a radical departure from the formality of Congregational services and attracted rich and poor alike. It wasn't until 1835 that the second meeting was held in Wesleyan Grove in Oak Bluffs. Revivalism began to sweep the island, and preachers approached their task with extraordinary zeal as they gathered converts away from the Congregationalists. Their fervor swelled the ranks of those who came to worship in the grove of oak trees.

As the Methodist movement soared, the visitors started pitching their tents in a circle around the speaker's podium. There were family tents and communal tents with partitions down the middle to separate the sexes. In the 1870s a circus-style tent was erected in the center of the Camp Ground for the meetings. This was replaced in 1879 by the present Tabernacle in the center of Trinity Park.

Camp meetings usually lasted about two weeks, but because many members found this seaside "watering spot" delightful, they began staying longer, and in 1864 the first of the "wooden tents" appeared. These tiny cottages, built on the tent sites, were as close together as the original tents, many not 2 feet apart. The building boom reached a feverish pitch in the 1870s, when each person tried to outdo the neighbors with Carpenter Gothic decor. The facades were gaily festooned with gables, turrets, spires, scrollwork under the eaves, tiny balconies, rococo verandas, high-pitched roofs, leaded cathedral windows, and intricately cut shingles. The owners painted their lacy valentines in vivid rainbow hues of purple, pink, sea green, blue, and yellow, making this Hansel-and-Gretel village a landmark in gingerbread architecture.

Meanwhile, more and more steamboats were advertising the delights of an island holiday, and the town grew rapidly as a resort for secular visitors who built cottages, shops, and hotels in the Circuit Avenue and Ocean Park area. Carpenters could scarcely keep up with the booming demands. Hordes of Methodists and vacationers poured off the boats, including cyclists in their club colors; families with trunks, bags, and croquet sets; and young men in straw hats and women in hoop skirts and bonnets.

It was a new era, and working-class people were now taking summer vacations, which were formerly the province of the wealthy. Unlike the aristocratic Edgartown and the commercial Vineyard Haven, Oak Bluffs was a resort and a Methodist meeting place for people from all walks of life. Huge wooden hotels, dance halls (where the song "Tivoli Girl" became a great favorite), a boardwalk, and a roller-skating rink sprang up. It became so lively that the Methodists, wishing to spare their flock the temptations brought by sinful secular visitors, built a 7-foot fence all around the Camp Ground. Evidently it wasn't high enough; the holiday spirit prevailed, so they lowered the fence. Not only did the two groups mingle, but one visitor was shocked to hear the strains of "Nearer My God to Thee" wafting out from the roller-skating rink. Croquet games in the Camp Ground reached such a feverish pitch that cheating by ministers' daughters was reported in the local paper.

To celebrate the closing of the religious meetings for the year, the Methodists held Illumination Night near the end of August. The origin of this tradition is obscure. During camp meetings each tent was required to keep a lantern lit at night, which, an observer explained, resembled "the celestial city's pearly gates whose translucence would manifest the beauty of the glorious light within." But it was land developers from outside the Camp Ground who first sponsored a gala Illumination in the summer of 1869 that really lit the place up. The tradition grew until Japanese lanterns hung from every tree, rail, and beam, flickering in a fairyland setting of tiny houses. A Japanese family who had opened a gift shop in Oak Bluffs in the 1870s influenced the decorative character of this annual event, which has continued now for over a century.

The decline of Oak Bluffs was almost as rapid as its escalation. The hurried overbuilding—in many instances, underfinanced—the financial panic of 1873, and the burning of hotels (suspected to be arson) in the 1890s all contributed to the town's economic demise. But the Camp Ground, while not attracting the hordes it had in the past, continued to attract the Methodists each summer in the little houses surrounding the Tabernacle. The houses have continued to be carefully maintained, sometimes by families of the original owners who have passed them down from generation to generation. They are filled to capacity during the summer. The center of town, which is filled with restaurants, shops, a few inns, movie theaters, and the Flying Horses carousel, continues to attract many vacationers, and it has grown rapidly in recent years.

You must leave your car near the traffic circle, as the only way to see this fascinating and unique town is on foot. Even bicycles are not permitted in the Camp Ground.

The tiny rainbow-colored cottages that encircle Trinity Park in Oak Bluffs.

1. The Flying Horses
Circuit Avenue

We'll begin our walking tour at the traffic circle at the foot of Circuit Avenue, which is Oak Bluffs' main street. The Flying Horses is one of the nation's oldest carousels. The handsome wooden horses were carved in 1876 by C. W. F. Dare in New York City and were brought by steamer to Oak Bluffs in 1884. The carousel is a great rainy-day favorite for children. Also, concessionaires in the old building sell souvenirs and cotton candy. The carousel has been listed on the National Register of Historic Places and belongs to the Martha's Vineyard Preservation Trust.

2. Trinity Park
The Campgrounds
Circuit Avenue

Take the town's main street, Circuit Avenue, which begins across from the carousel. Just past the Oak Bluffs Pharmacy, on your right you'll see a sign and the main entrance into the Camp Ground. Immediately in front of you, in the center of the green is the large Tabernacle, encircled by a sidewalk and tiny houses. It was erected in 1879 to replace the original meeting tent. Constructed of T-irons, angle irons, pipe, and wooden rafters supporting a corrugated roof, it is one of the largest wrought-iron structures in the United States. Like many sections of the Camp Ground, the Tabernacle is listed in the National Register of Historic Places. Bear right here and circle the Camp Ground in a counterclockwise direction.

The Trinity Methodist Church, the only other building inside the large grassy circle, was built in 1878. Its outstanding feature is the stained-glass cathedral windows. Walk around this fairy-tale setting of gingerbread houses in rainbow colors, each with its wedding-cake trim. Notice one with heart-shaped cutouts, others with scrollwork, cathedral windows, and little spires. They are painted lavender and white, green and orange, yellow and purple, blue and white, and any other combination that highlights the myriad forms of gingerbread. As you stroll around the circle, take time to walk a few steps down the lanes that radiate from the green; they are filled with these tiny "wooden tents."

Return to Circuit Avenue the same way you entered.

3. Union Chapel
Circuit Avenue

Turn right on Circuit Avenue for a few steps, and go directly across the street to the Union Chapel. Built in 1871 during the heyday of the Oak Bluffs land boom, it was for those secular souls who lived outside the Camp Ground's 7-foot fence. "When complete with the spire reaching an altitude of 96 feet," the paper reported, "it will overtop everything." This nondenominational, octagonal chapel with a domed ceiling has a balcony around five sides and eight triangular windows emerging from the roof like spired dormers. The chapel's consecration was the highlight of a series of festive events that year: the completion of the island's first (and only) drawbridge over the lagoon and the arrival of a new paddle-wheel steamer. The Vineyard Haven band played a new composition especially written to commemorate Tisbury's independence from West Tisbury, called "The Bartholomew Gosnold Quickstep"!

4. Ocean Park

Behind the Union Chapel, go left on Grove Avenue to Ocean Avenue and continue along to Ocean Park. Stay on this side of the park, which is fringed with large, yet dainty, gingerbread cottages. A band holds evening concerts in the charming gazebo in the center of the park.

As you continue toward the waterfront, the Episcopal Church is on your left, at the intersection of several roads. A Civil War monument is on the right. This statue of a Confederate soldier, painted in lifelike colors and looking like a toy soldier, was commissioned by a Southerner who had moved to the island. It is reputed to be the only such monument erected right after the war by a member of the Confederacy. The plaque reads, "The chasm is closed," and it is dedicated to "the Union veterans of the Civil War and patriotic citizens of Martha's Vineyard in honor of Confederate soldiers."

5. Beach and Harbor

Continue past the monument to the waterfront where the Oak Bluffs Public Beach runs along both sides of the steamship wharf. The area here and back toward the Flying Horses and the traffic circle was once the site of a huge hotel, the roller-skating rink, a dance hall called The Tivoli ("I lov it" spelled backward), and the terminus for the island's only train, the Active, which ran from Oak Bluffs to South Beach via Edgartown for a number of years. When the hotel burned down along

Weekly concerts are held in the gazebo in Ocean Park, which is surrounded by large, carpenter-gothic homes.

with the Active's turnstile, the train continued to run—forwards to Edgartown and backwards to Oak Bluffs!

Continue along the waterfront toward Oak Bluffs Harbor. You'll pass the public beach and stone jetty marking the entrance to Oak Bluffs Harbor and the pier where ferries from the Cape are docked. A short distance ahead the street terminates at the traffic circle by the Flying Horses, where the walking tour began.

6. Alongshore to Edgartown

Leaving Oak Bluffs for Edgartown along Seaview Avenue, there's a small settlement of houses and an artificially created harbor on the outskirts of Oak Bluffs. Called Harthaven, it is named for the family that originally settled here, and many of the cottages are still owned by members of the Hart family.

Just beyond Harthaven is the beginning of the Joseph A. Sylvia Beach, also called State Beach, which is one of the best swimming beaches on the island. The large body of inland water on your right is Sengekontacket Pond, a favorite spot for bird watchers and a popular scalloping area for Vineyard fishing crews in the winter months.

As you continue past the beach and enter the outskirts of Edgartown, there is a fork in the road where the inland road back to Vineyard Haven branches off.

There is a convenient parking lot here plus bus service to the center of Edgartown and out to the ocean at South Beach. There is another public parking lot at the Edgartown Grammar School. You will want to park your car before touring Edgartown.

14

EDGARTOWN TOUR

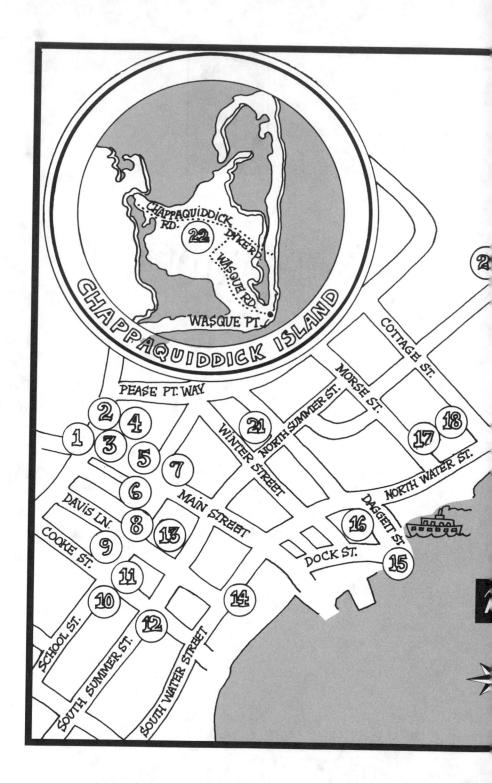

Edgartown

Points of Interest

1. START OF TOUR
2. CAPTAIN THOMAS MELLEN HOUSE
3. DR. DANIEL FISHER HOUSE
4. VINCENT HOUSE
5. OLD WHALING CHURCH
6. ST. ELIZABETH'S CHURCH
7. DUKES COUNTY COURT HOUSE
8. FORMER MASONIC HALL
9. THAXTER ACADEMY
10. THE VINEYARD MUSEUM
11. COOKE & SCHOOL STREETS
12. FIRST FEDERATED CHURCH
13. VINEYARD GAZETTE OFFICE
14. PAGODA TREE
15. DOCK & CHAPPAQUIDDICK FERRY
16. OLD SCULPIN ART GALLERY
17. JOHN O. MORSE HOUSE
18. CAPTAIN'S HOUSE
19. THE LIGHTHOUSE
20. EMILY POST HOUSE
21. ST. ANDREW'S CHURCH
22. CHAPPAQUIDDICK ISLAND

The first white settlement on Martha's Vineyard was located in Edgartown in 1642. Called Great Harbor by the early settlers, it was a self-sufficient little farming and fishing community. Lacking in trade goods and isolated from maritime traffic moving through Vineyard Sound, the village grew very slowly; it had only thirty-six houses in 1694. But with the gradual increase in island exports and the growth of offshore whaling, the port grew in importance until it reached its peak of prosperity in the nineteenth century.

Just before the American Revolution, Nantucket and Martha's Vineyard owned about one-quarter of America's whaling fleet. Many vessels were commandeered or sunk by the British during the war, and Edgartown's fleet suffered heavy losses. There was a thirty-year hiatus in the local whaling industry, but eventually the fleet was rebuilt, and from about 1820 to the Civil War—a time when many of Edgartown's handsome houses were built—whaling was in its prime. From Greenland to South America, from the Indian Ocean, around the Horn, to the Pacific and Bering Sea, Edgartown's ships sailed on three- and four-year voyages in pursuit of the mammals whose oil and whalebone (the latter used for women's corsets) meant instant riches.

Edgartown provisioned its own fleet and, for a time, that of Nantucket when the large, deep-draft ships needed for long voyages could not get over the sand bar at the entrance to Nantucket Harbor. Nantucket had once been the whaling capital of the world (a title later bestowed on New Bedford); Edgartown's fleet was smaller but prospered well. The wharves along the waterfront were piled high with barrels of oil where whaleships were tied up to unload or to fit out for another long voyage. A bakery turned out hardtack, one of the staples aboard ship. Sail lofts, cooperages, cordwainers, weavers, hat makers, and a tannery were crowded together on Dock Street along with the glowing forges of smithies. The tangy salt air was tinged with the smells of hot metal, sperm oil, rigging tar, and hemp. Young and old were lured to the waterfront, where there were social activities, tales of extraordinary voyages, jobs, excitement, and prospects of wealth.

When the whaling era ended, Edgartown continued to have a very active fishing fleet. The town got its start as a summer resort when a hotel was built at Katama in 1872. This venture didn't last; but just as Bostonians discovered West Chop, New Yorkers found Edgartown and its handsome houses very charming. Some, following Emily Post's lead, brought strict social mores, and for generations they influenced the reserved character of the community. New Yorkers were joined in Edgartown by people from New Jersey and Philadelphia. Changes came slowly to Edgartown until the 1980s, when many new inns, restaurants, snack shops, and gift shops were introduced in the downtown area. Fortunately, two or three blocks from the center in any direction you will find attractive houses that keep the town from losing its original character, and it is surprisingly quiet, in spite of the traffic.

Edgartown has narrow streets, and the large houses are built close together, which was common in many New England seaports where the town was built around a harbor. The best way to see the town is a walking tour, and a stroll through the town, day or night, is a delight. It is a tradition in many New England villages to name the houses after the original owner or, in some cases, a famous occupant. You will find many houses on this tour referred to in that manner. There are other fine houses not mentioned, but if you are aware of various architectural periods, you can date the houses yourself as you stroll along.

One additional helpful note: Across Church Street from the back of the Old Whaling Church is the Edgartown Visitors' Center. In addition to providing valuable information, the center houses a post office and public rest rooms. Shuttle buses from Vineyard Haven and Oak Bluffs terminate here as do several chartered bus tours.

1. Start of Tour

We will begin the tour at the intersection of Upper Main Street and Pease Point Way by the flagpole and the memorial to World War II veterans. You are a block from the center here.

2. Captain Thomas Mellen House
Main Street

The gray house on your left at the corner of Pease Point Way and Main Street was the home of Captain Mellen, master of the ship *Levi Starbuck*, which was captured and burned in the Civil War. He was also captain of the *Europa*, one of the ships that rescued 224 sailors in the Bering Sea in 1871. America's whaling fleet had become unexpectedly trapped in the ice, and it was thought the men would die from starvation and cold long before rescue vessels could reach them. Fortunately, ships were able to get through, thus avoiding what would have been the greatest disaster in America's whaling industry. This foursquare, nineteenth-century house with a columned doorway has had the front windows changed, but those on the back wing still have the twelve-over-twelve panes. It has a central hallway plan.

3. Dr. Daniel Fisher House
Main Street

The next house on your left is Dr. Fisher's handsome transitional house, built in 1840, with the Greek Revival portico and intricately carved roof rail of the Federal period. The town's most successful and versatile businessperson at the time, Dr. Fisher supplied whale oil to many United States lighthouses. He also owned a large spermaceti candle factory on the waterfront, a hardtack bakery, and the town dock. He founded the Martha's Vineyard National Bank, operated a flour mill in North Tisbury, and practiced medicine! When it came to building his house, Dr. Fisher hired a Boston architect and insisted on the finest materials. It was framed with timbers of Maine pine that had been soaked in lime for two years and was constructed entirely with brass and copper nails. From the enclosed cupola he could look far out to sea and observe the comings and goings of vessels during the height of the whaling era.

The richly carved balustrade around the roof and porch, as well as the beautiful portico, make it one of the two most elegant structures in town. It is now owned by Martha's Vineyard Preservation Trust. The trust was formed to save, restore, and make self-sufficient any important island buildings that might otherwise be sold for commercial purposes or radically remodeled. The Fisher house, one of six belonging to the trust, is beautifully decorated and open to the public for parties.

4. The Vincent House
Main Street

On the spacious lawn behind the Fisher house is an old farmhouse also owned by the Martha's Vineyard Preservation Trust and open to the public. One of the oldest houses on the island (circa 1675), it was moved to its present site from the Great Plain area outside of Edgartown on the south shore. It's a fine example of a one-story full Cape, with two windows on either side of the front door, a huge central chimney with three fireplaces, and tiny stairs to the attic. The steep shed roof, flush with the windows, acts as both roof and wall, and the small ell was added at a later date. The house's present windows replaced the original diamond-shaped leaded lights. The changes and additions made to the house by various owners in the course of 300 years remain.

The building exemplifies for the public how these early houses were constructed; there are sections of wall left open and unfinished to show how the "wattle and daub" clay infilling was constructed. It is open to the public in the summer.

5. The Old Whaling Church
Main Street

Continuing down Main Street, the next building on your left is the huge Methodist Church, more often called the Old Whaling Church because it was built with whaling money in 1843. The lumber was brought down from Maine by Captain John Morse in his schooner. The magnificent organ was installed in 1869, and before the clock was built there were four handsome Gothic windows. The church is the island's outstanding example of Greek Revival architecture. The enormous Gothic columns are its most distinctive feature, along with its 92-foot-high tower. The light in the steeple, once a beacon to sailors, can be seen by ships many miles at sea.

The church has long been an island landmark, but a rapidly diminishing Methodist congregation put the building's future in jeopardy until it was given to the Martha's Vineyard Preservation Trust. Funds were raised for its restoration, and it is now a performing arts center. Church services are held on Sundays during the summer months only.

6. St. Elizabeth's Church
Main Street

Diagonally across the street from the Old Whaling Church is the Catholic church. Although the Portuguese had been coming to the island from the Azores since Revolutionary times, Catholicism was not established here until much later. The first Catholic church was built in Oak Bluffs in 1880, and St. Elizabeth's was built in 1925.

7. Dukes County Court House
Main Street

The next building on your left is the courthouse, built in 1858 and one of the first brick buildings constructed on the island. Originally the jailhouse was also here, but it was torn down in 1870 when the new jail and jailer's house were built farther up Main Street. All the county's business is conducted here, including sessions of the Superior Court each spring and fall.

8. Former Masonic Hall
School Street

Directly in front of the courthouse, across Main Street, take School Street. Just past the back of St. Elizabeth's Church, on your right, is a

Historic North Water Street in Edgartown, which is lined with beautiful nineteenth-century houses built with whaling money.

large columned building, the former Masonic Hall. It was built in 1839 as a Baptist church, but when the Baptists and Congregationalists united to form the Federated Church on South Summer Street, this building was taken over by the Masonic Lodge. It is now a private home.

9. Thaxter Academy
School Street

Continue down School Street and cross Davis Lane. Notice the handsome building on your right, at the corner. It was formerly a private school and is now a private home. It was built by Leavitt Thaxter, son of the minister of the Congregational Church, after he returned from sea and a teaching career in Massachusetts and Georgia. With his father's help, he built the academy. The classic form of the doorway is particularly handsome.

10. The Vineyard Museum
   School and Cooke Streets

Continue on down School Street and at the corner you will see the grounds and buildings of the Vineyard Museum. This is the major historical center on the island; it houses the island's archives and many Colonial artifacts. It has more than one hundred whaling vessel logbooks covering the period of the island's greatest prosperity from that industry.

The Thomas Cooke house was built in 1765 for Squire Cooke, a businessman, politician, justice, and collector of customs from 1784 through 1786. It is an exceptional example of a pre–Revolutionary War house, having had almost no modifications since the 1850s.

Out on the lawn is the magnificent, enormous Fresnel lens from the old Gay Head Lighthouse. Mounted in a replica of the watch room and lantern of the 1856 lighthouse, this French lens is a national treasure. One of very few extant, it is lit every night and is operated Sunday evenings in July and August, rotating as it originally did. There is an exhibition of its history in the watch room under the lens. Behind the light is a boat shed with some fascinating exhibits. The main building houses the Francis Foster Museum and the Gale Huntington Library of History. Next door, the Captain Francis Pease house has an art gallery, displays of Indian artifacts, and other exhibits. All the buildings are open to the public. (See museums in Chapter 9.)

11. Intersection of Cooke and School Streets

The three private houses opposite the entrance to the Vineyard Museum are fine examples of different types of architecture.

The small farmhouse, circa 1720, is typical of many early Vineyard houses and was moved by oxen to its present location. The large, handsome Captain Thomas Cooke house, across School Street, has two end chimneys and a central hall, which was popular in the late eighteenth century. Squire Cooke built this house for himself and gave his house on the museum grounds to his son at the time of his son's marriage. The small house diagonally across from the museum's entrance was built in 1820 by Captain Jethro Ripley, owner of a coasting schooner, who moved freight under sail for years.

The Dr. Daniel Fisher House shows the delicate details of the Federal
period. (top)

The office of the Vineyard Gazette is located in a pre-Revolutionary house on
South Summer Street. (bottom)

The famous Old Whaling Church decorated for Christmas. It is now the
island's performing arts center. (right)

12. First Federated Church
South Summer and Cooke Streets

Proceed down Cooke Street 1 block toward the waterfront to the corner of Cooke and South Summer streets. The church here was originally built as a Congregational Church in 1828, but it merged with the Baptist Church a century later and became the Federated Church. It is a beautifully designed structure, and the interior contains old box pews as well as a Hook and Hastings organ. The chandelier has the original whale oil lamps, and the church clock is one of the earliest bearing the name Ingraham. At night, the light in the graceful and delicate steeple can be seen far out at sea. The parish house next door is an old schoolhouse that was moved here in 1850.

13. The Vineyard Gazette Office
South Summer Street

Continue on South Summer Street toward Main Street. At the corner of Davis Lane is the main office of the *Vineyard Gazette,* a nationally known, award-winning weekly newspaper that has been in existence for 138 years. It is located in a house built by Captain Benjamin Smith in 1764. It was at one time a home for the poor, and the four rooms, each with a fireplace, accommodated four indigent families. A large addition has been constructed on the back of the building to accommodate the growing staff of the paper, while the interior of the original structure has been carefully preserved.

Henry Beetle Hough, the late author and editor, and his wife, Elizabeth Bowie Hough, owned and published the paper for forty-eight years until Hough sold it to James Reston of the *New York Times* in 1968. His son, Richard Reston, is the editor and publisher. Hough continued writing the editorials until his death in 1984. Because of his lifelong crusade to preserve the natural beauty of the island, Hough was known as "the conscience of Martha's Vineyard."

14. Pagoda Tree
South Water Street

Follow Davis Lane 1 block toward the waterfront to South Water Street. Turn left and head back toward Main Street, but as you do, be sure to notice the fine whaling captains' houses in this area. Their doorways, roof walks, and balustrades illustrate the Colonial, Federal, Greek Revival, and Victorian periods of architecture. In the middle of the block, on the right, is the huge Pagoda Tree. The tree was brought from China in a flowerpot by Captain Thomas Milton to plant beside his new home, now part of the Harborside Inn complex. Captain Milton first put in to Edgartown Harbor while serving aboard the privateer *Yankee* in the War of 1812. He liked the town so much that he bought this house lot in 1814 and some years later built the house at a cost of $900.

15. Town Dock and Chappaquidick Ferry
   Dock Street

At the corner of Main Street, turn right and head down toward the waterfront. The town parking lot and the Edgartown Yacht Club are straight ahead, but bear left along Dock Street. During the whaling era this was where the shops catering to the whaling industry were clustered together. Ship chandlers supplied whaleships tied up at the docks, where barrels of oil for Dr. Daniel Fisher's whale oil factory were stacked.

Dr. Fisher also owned the town dock, now called Memorial Wharf. Today it is used by Edgartown's small fishing fleet; also, it is the termination point of the Memorial Day parade where schoolchildren toss flowers into the harbor in memory of island residents who were lost at sea.

Beside the dock are the ferries to Chappaquiddick, called *On Time I, II,* and *III* because they have no time schedule. The first ferry was actually a rowboat, and freight was floated across on a barge.

16. Old Sculpin Art Gallery
   Dock Street

Across from the town dock is the art gallery. This building was part of Dr. Daniel Fisher's whale oil refinery and was later on a feed mill. Its facade has not changed except for the small tower. In the early 1900s it became Manuel Swartz Roberts' boat shop, where he built catboats, which are small, gaff-rigged sailboats. They were beautifully constructed and became extremely popular. Summer visitors, island residents, and yacht sailors frequented his shop to admire the furniture and decoys he made as well as the boats.

The gallery is open all summer and shows the work of a series of interesting artists. The interior retains its old, weathered beams and uneven, pockmarked floor. The only modern addition is the pegboard on the walls necessary for hanging paintings.

North Water Street

Walk up Daggett Street to the end and turn right on North Water Street. The Daggett House on this corner, built in 1750, is the only pre–Revolutionary hip-roof house in the village. All along the street you will see some of the best examples of Colonial, Federal, and Greek Revival architecture on the island; many of them were built by shipwrights without the benefit of architects. These independent Yankees took all the liberties they liked with the prevailing styles, and modest adaptations of the purer forms are apparent in the roof, doorway, portico, window, and chimney arrangements.

Just past the Daggett House and across the street, three Colonial houses with Georgian adornments are set at a slight angle so the owners could see vessels rounding Cape Pogue on Chappaquiddick.

There are a number of very elegant houses with handsome facades along this street. Take time to walk slowly and study their architectural details. Number 68 North Water Street, built in 1784, has one of the handsomest doorways in town.

17. The John O. Morse House
Morse and North Water Streets

Just after you cross Morse Street, notice the large house on your left, the Morse house. It was built in 1840 at the height of the whaling era. Captain Morse owned a large commercial wharf down on the waterfront, just below the house, where the shipyard is now located. He was master of the whaleship *Hector,* known as "the luckiest whaleship afloat." Not only did he have "greasy luck," but he survived a battle with a sperm whale when the mammal took the captain's boat in his mouth, held it on end, and shook it to pieces. He survived, and from another whaleboat he buried his lance in the whale. During the height of the gold rush in 1849, he took time out from whaling to sail a group of men around the Horn to California in his bark, *Sarah.*

The original house had a porch on the first floor, looking seaward; the second-story porch was added at a later date. Some details on the facade reflect the earlier Federal period, while the heavy columns date to the Greek Revival period.

18. The Captain's House
North Water Street

As you continue on North Water Street, the next house on your left vies with the Dr. Daniel Fisher House as the most magnificent Federal mansion on the island, although they both have Greek Revival porticos. Built in 1832 for Captain George Lawrence and sold, almost immediately, to Captain Jared Fisher, it represented the height of luxury for the time. It features Romanesque design with narrow sidelights, slender columns, gracefully carved balusters, and detailed trim on the roof walk typical of the Federal period. Inside it has beautiful details on the ceilings, mantelpieces, and moldings.

Jared Fisher's granddaughter married into the Bliss family of Boston, and the house remained in the family for five generations before it was given to the Society for the Preservation of New England Antiquities. It is not open to the public. Notice the mannequin of a woman on the roof walk, holding a spyglass and gazing out to sea over Chappaquiddick Island. It is a reminder of the women who searched for whaleships returning from the Pacific after several years' voyage.

19. The Lighthouse

Continuing along North Water Street you pass by Cottage Street. It was in this area that Dr. Daniel Fisher had his spermaceti candle factory.

A little farther along you come to the path leading down to the automated lighthouse at the entrance to Edgartown Harbor and the beach. Where the lighthouse now stands, there was once a lighthouse keeper's house with a light tower on top. To reach it in those days, there was a long, wooden bridge over the marshy land to the beach. It was known as the "Bridge of Sighs" because young men used to take their dates for romantic evening strolls out to the beach.

Just up the street from the path, the house on your left next to the hotel has a Dutch gambrel roof, which is very rare in Vineyard architecture.

20. Emily Post House
Fuller Street

Continue past the hotel. From here the road curves around the bluff and is called Starbuck Neck. The houses fronting the outer harbor are typical, large, shingled, turn-of-the-century summer cottages. Starbuck Neck dead-ends at Fuller Street. Turn left here and head back toward the center of town. The second house on your right, past the two tennis courts, is the Emily Post House with its beautiful garden. Considered the social arbiter of her day, Emily Post influenced the elite character of the town for years.

Weekly sailing races start near the lighthouse in Edgartown. Chappaquiddick Island is in the background.

21. Saint Andrew's Church
North Summer and Winter Streets

Continue straight ahead on Fuller Street to the end, turn right on Morse Street for half a block, and turn left onto North Summer Street. At the corner of Winter Street is the lovely, ivy-covered Episcopal Church. The cornerstone for the church was laid in 1899, and before that services were held in a room over a dry goods store on Main Street.

Diagonally across the street is a very fine example of an eighteenth-century half-Cape house; the dormers were a later addition. Across the street from the back of the church is one of the best examples of a Greek Revival house in Edgartown.

At the end of the block you are back on Main Street, and 2 blocks up to your right is where the tour began at the corner of Pease Point Way.

22. Chappaquiddick Island

If you wish, return to the town dock where you can take the ferry to Chappaquiddick.

It is difficult to see Chappy on foot unless you plan to take the whole day, because the main attraction is the beach on the far side of the island, 3 miles away. When you leave the ferry, stay on the hard-surfaced road past the private Chappaquiddick Beach Club on your left, and continue up the hill. The road meanders by scrub oak, pine, and masses of grapevines; it passes a gas station, the only commercial building on the island, and a new community center for island residents, then comes to a sharp right-hand curve.

If you follow the paved road, it leads to Wasque Point, a wildlife reservation along the beach. There are signs directing the visitor to parking areas. Standing on this point, which is the southern tip of Chappaquiddick, and facing the sea, you can see the long sand spit on your right that connects the island with the Katama end of Edgartown at South Beach. Over the years the sea has broken through the barrier beach and separated the two islands during a hurricane or severe winter storm, and in time the ocean and currents build it up and close off the opening.

To visit Chappaquiddick Island, take the ferry from the town dock in Edgartown.

The late Henry Hough's family boathouse stands on the island's north shore adjacent to Cedar Tree Neck.

As you return to the ferry, you'll notice driveways leading to private homes. It wasn't until the middle of the eighteenth century that Chappaquiddick Island had any white settlers. Prior to that it was an Indian settlement and one of four sachemships on Martha's Vineyard. In an Indian dialect, Chappaquiddick meant "The Separated Island." When some of Edgartown's residents moved here, they engaged in shellfishing and raising corn, the island's principal livelihoods. Corn was exported to Maine and bartered for cedar posts to fence the cattle grazing on the open land. But the majority of residents were sea captains, and in 1878 a census listed forty-two—probably the highest number of sea captains in any community that size.

One resident, who was part owner of the island's corn gristmill, was also a patent medicine king. Perry Davis started the manufacture of his Vegetable Pain Killer here. Its chief ingredients, however, were alcohol and opium, and it immediately became so successful he moved his whole operation to Providence.

At one time there was a semaphore signal on Sampson's Hill, the highest point of land on the island. This was also where the Indians kept a lookout for whales and where the Humane Society boat was launched into the surf to go to the aid of vessels in distress on Muskeget Shoals. Before the Coast Guard began operating, there were lookouts fringing the island at strategic points with the Humane Society's boats ready to be launched on a moment's notice.

The Chappaquiddick Indians were not treated well, and they were segregated in the North Neck area on poor land. Several Edgartownians tried to help them, but their help was late in coming; those who did survive poverty and the white settlers' diseases moved to Gay Head or Cape Cod.

15

UP-ISLAND
TOUR

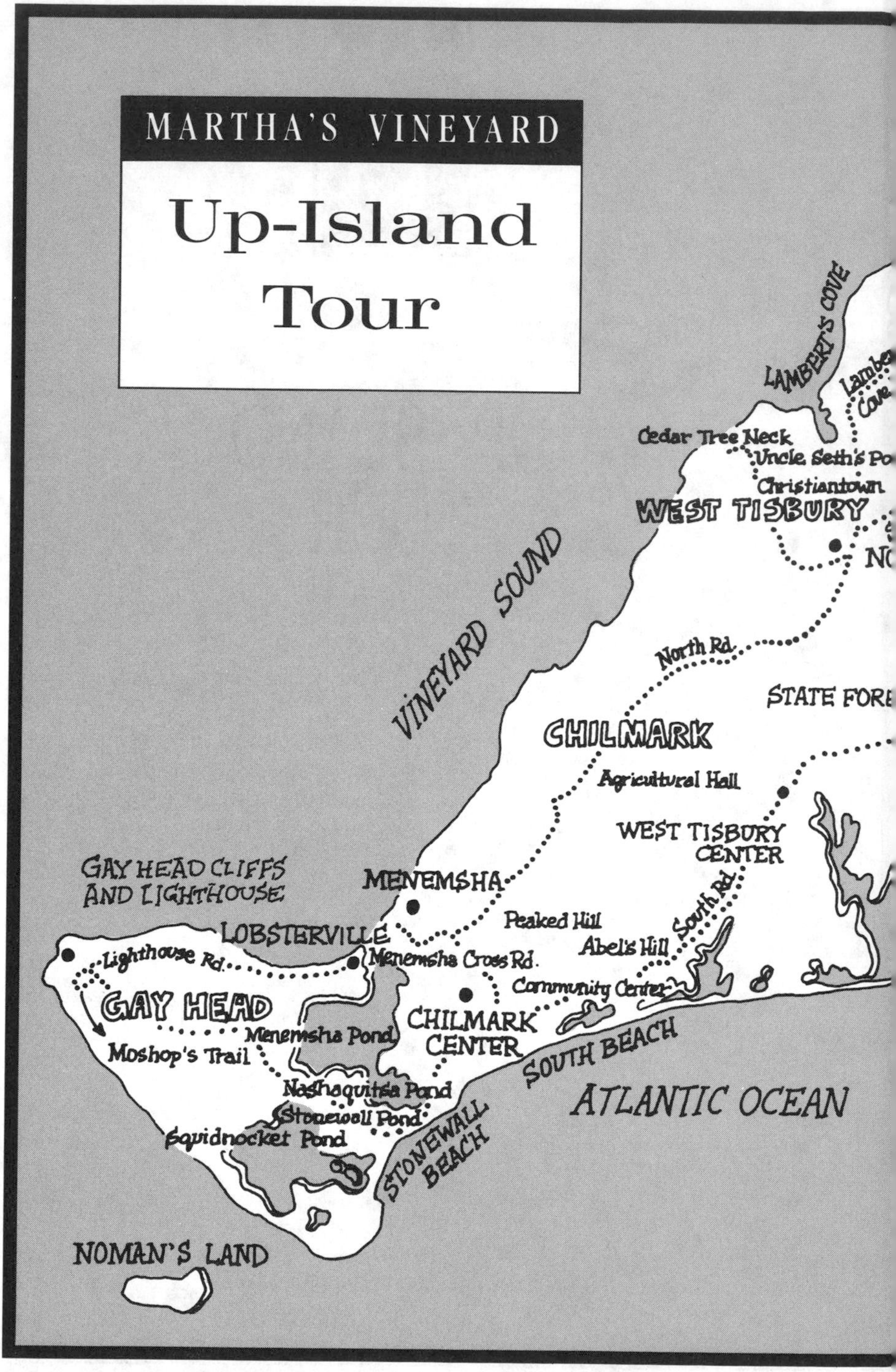

Up-Island Tour

LAMBERT'S COVE

Lambert's Cove

Cedar Tree Neck

Uncle Seth's Po

Christiantown

WEST TISBURY

NO

VINEYARD SOUND

North Rd.

STATE FORE

CHILMARK

Agricultural Hall

WEST TISBURY CENTER

GAY HEAD CLIFFS AND LIGHTHOUSE

MENEMSHA

Peaked Hill

LOBSTERVILLE

Menemsha Cross Rd.

Abel's Hill

South Rd.

Lighthouse Rd.

Community Center

GAY HEAD

Menemsha Pond

CHILMARK CENTER

Moshop's Trail

SOUTH BEACH

Nashaquitsa Pond

Stonewall Pond

ATLANTIC OCEAN

Squidnocket Pond

STONEWALL BEACH

NOMAN'S LAND

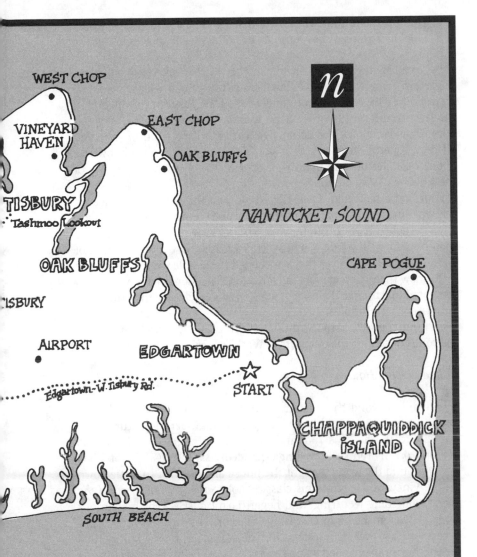

This Up-Island tour will take about two and a half hours, which includes stops of ten minutes or so at various places along the way.

Begin at Memorial Park on upper Main Street on the outskirts of Edgartown, where the West Tisbury–Edgartown Road is clearly marked on the signs. This road was originally called the Takemmy Trail, and in the seventeenth century it led to an Indian village on the shores of Tisbury Great Pond near the ocean. The road is inland from the sea, and all the property on your left as you drive along is privately owned. About 2½ miles out of Edgartown, on your right, is the beginning of the 4,000-acre state forest.

Four and a half miles from Edgartown, on the left, is the Place on the Wayside, a stone marker in memory of Thomas Mayhew, Jr., who often preached here to the Indians. The Indians placed stones on the spot in memory of young Mayhew, who was the most compassionate of all the Mayhews, and over the years added to the pile when they passed by to show their appreciation and affection. The stones have since been cemented together, and a bronze marker was erected by the Daughters of the American Revolution.

Continue past the airport, the road into Scrubby Neck Stables, and the youth hostel, on the outskirts of West Tisbury.

Joshua Slocum House

A half mile beyond the hostel, on your left, is the Joshua Slocum house, an unusual example of a very early eighteenth-century Cape house with its sag-back roof and overhang. In 1898 Captain Joshua Slocum, on his return from single-handedly sailing his 36-foot sloop *Spray* around the world, bought the house and planned to settle down on the Vineyard. He wrote his classic book, *Sailing Alone Around the World*, did some lecturing, and began farming. He kept his famous sloop at Menemsha or in Oak Bluffs Harbor. His farming proved unsuccessful, however, and restless for the sea again, he set sail in 1907 for another single-handed voyage and was never heard from again.

Mill Pond

At the Mill Pond, the tiny building on your right was once a grammar school and later an ice house; it is now West Tisbury's Police Department. The mill itself dates back to the early part of the eighteenth century and was a factory for the manufacture of satinet, a heavy woolen fabric made from sheep's wool that was used for whaler's pea jackets. It is now the headquarters for the Martha's Vineyard Garden Club. The pond is a fun place for children to feed the ducks and swans.

West Tisbury Center

At the "T" intersection ahead, the road to your right leads past the West Tisbury cemetery to North Tisbury and back toward Vineyard Haven. Bear left to continue Up-Island along the shore on South Road. A charming, rural farming village in mid-island, West Tisbury was incorporated in 1671 and seems miles from the sea, but its boundaries cut a wide, north-south swath through the middle of the island. Horseback riding is very popular on the trails through woodlands, open fields, and alongshore. The old village store bears the advertisement, "Dealers In Almost Everything." The handsome Congregational Church stands on the corner of Music Street, which got its name a hundred years ago when every house on the street was reputed to have a piano.

Across Music Street from the church is the mansard-roofed town hall, which, until recently, was the elementary school. In the nineteenth century it was a coeducational school called the Dukes County Academy and was attended by local and mainland children. Whalers also attended classes here to brush up on schooling they'd missed because they went to sea at an early age.

The building beyond the school is the Agricultural Hall, where the farmers' market was held on Saturdays all summer.

Chilmark

A half mile beyond West Tisbury's center is the town line of Chilmark. This is a town of hills, with stone walls rolling over the moors and reaching down to the sea, clumps of scrub oak and pine sculpted close to the ground by the relentless winds, wildflowers, and windswept beaches. Old Vineyard houses as well as very modern ones dot the landscape and the spiky Scotch Broom bursts into a brilliant yellow on the moors in June. Green ribbons of marsh fringe the tidal ponds, and from the high, rolling hills there are spectacular views of Vineyard Sound and the great sweep of the Atlantic Ocean.

Incorporated in 1694, and, like Tisbury, named for its parent town in England, Chilmark began as a fishing and farming community like other island villages. Great flocks of sheep roamed the moors, and the placement of houses reflected a feudal system of sheep farming on communally held property. Houses were sparsely scattered over the hillsides, unlike the Down-Island towns, where they were clustered together around the waterfront.

Fifty students in kindergarten through fifth grade attend the Chilmark School in Beetlebung Corner, which was built in 1860.

Abel's Hill

The South Road meanders along through the countryside, becoming more hilly as it reaches a summit at Abel's Hill, named for an Indian whose wigwam once stood on this spot. The Chilmark cemetery has some unusual old gravestones and some famous new ones. Both comedian John Belushi and author Lillian Hellman are buried here. Up behind it is an Indian cemetery with fieldstones to mark the graves, the very small stones indicating a child. While the cemetery can be visited, it is now against the law to make rubbings of these gravestones.

Chilmark Center

Two miles farther along, after passing over the little Fulling Mill Brook, which was once the site of a mill for thickening homemade woolen cloth, the road winds up a hill where open, rolling fields touch the sea. There is a dirt road on the left that leads to the Lucy Vincent Beach, which is for Chilmark residents and guests only. Just before this road, on the right, there's an old full-Cape house framed with a magnificent stone wall, which has its place in Up-Island history.

Called Barn House, it was started in 1920 as a private inn. The main house was used for meals. The chicken coops and outbuildings were converted into living quarters and the large barn was fixed up for social gatherings. Barn House was organized by a group of extreme liberals, some of Marxist and Communist persuasion, who summered here with their families. In the ensuing years such well-known figures as the Socialist Norman Thomas; Roger Baldwin, the founder of the American Civil Liberties Union; Felix Frankfurter, who went on to become a Supreme Court justice; and the journalist Walter Lippmann visited with the Barn House's founder, Stanley King, who was president of Amherst College at the time. The Vineyarders called Barn House "that hangout for radicals."

There were others in the arts who came here in the twenties and thirties, not only because they preferred Chilmark's sparsely settled, rural character, but also because it was often all they could afford. A fish house or barn might be rented for $25 for the summer. The informality and social gatherings, which in those days included summer and year-round residents, appealed to people in the arts.

Just before the intersection, which is the center of Chilmark, is the Community Center on your left, which is the gathering place for Chilmark residents. This intersection was named Beetlebung Corner for the grove of beetlebung trees (a local term for tupelos) on your right, which are enclosed with a split-rail fence. The wood from these oriental-looking trees, whose leaves turn a fiery red in the fall, is extremely tough, and for years it was used to make wooden mallets (beetles) and bungs to plug the bungholes of wooden casks and barrels.

Chilmark Center has a two-room schoolhouse still in use; except for a new addition, it looks the same as it did in 1860, when it was illustrated in *Harper's* magazine. The town hall, firehouse, several stores, and delicately spired Methodist church complete this rural village. In 1828 this church was moved from Edgartown to the Middle Road, and in 1915 to its present location where Roger Allen, a highly respected town official who was a superb carpenter, built the steeple.

On the road to Gay Head

Three roads converge at the center of Chilmark; Middle Road, to your right, goes back to Music Street in West Tisbury; Menemsha Cross Road, straight ahead, goes to Chilmark's port; and the South Road, to your left, continues on to Gay Head.

Bear left on the South Road. A mile farther along there's a bridge, the only link to this end of the island. There is a boat ramp on your right into Nashaquitsa Pond, and Stonewall Pond is on the left. A tenth of a mile beyond, the stone enclosure on the left is an old cattle pound that was used for stray cows and sheep when thousands roamed the moors.

The road winds up a hill to the lookout, which affords a spectacular view of Nashaquitsa and Menemsha ponds, dotted with white sails, and hillside farmhouses weathered to a silvery gray. Beyond the ponds is Menemsha, and across Vineyard Sound the Elizabeth Islands stand out on a clear day.

The hilly road winds around the Gay Head town line at Herring Creek. In the eighteenth and nineteenth centuries, herring was very important to the island's economy. They were seined out of many island creeks when they swam up into ponds in the spring to spawn. The fish were pickled in barrels for export, salted, smoked, or used for cod and lobster bait. Later the scales were sold for making "Priscilla pearls."

At the creek the small, gray house fronting on Menemsha Pond, to your right, belonged to the Missouri artist Thomas Hart Benton, who was renowned for his many murals, including one in the Truman Library. The Bentons summered on the island for fifty-five years.

Gay Head

Continue straight on the South Road to the Gay Head Cliffs. Gay Head is as famous for its cliffs, now a National Landmark, as it is for its people. Both are deserving of their place in history. Gay Head is one of the two Indian townships in the state of Massachusetts (Mashpee is the other). The town was incorporated in 1870, and the Indians were merged in the general community with all the "rights and privileges and with all the duties and liabilities of citizens."

Prior to then, the town was part of Chilmark. The Indians had always willingly shared their knowledge of fishing and planting crops, including the way to steam fish and shellfish on a beach (the origin of the clambake). In turn, the white settlers' efforts to Christianize and educate the Indians were well rewarded when one Gay Header went to Harvard as early as 1665, and another served in the state legislature in the nineteenth century. The Indians lived in loosely constructed wigwams covered with mats woven of marsh grasses. They moved from place to place, not only to let the soil rest, but also to take advantage of coastal and inland climates. They lived alongshore in warmer months and moved back into the woods and valleys in winter.

The Indians were extremely able, courageous sailors, and because it was considered good luck to have a Gay Header aboard, they were in great demand as helmsmen on whaleships. It was the coxswain in the longboat who cast the first iron into the whale. They attained immortality as whalers through Tashtego, the Gay Head Indian in Herman Melville's classic, *Moby Dick*. Another who gained local renown was Amos Smalley, the only Vineyarder known to have harpooned a white whale.

A cluster of houses alongside the main road is the village center; the former one-room schoolhouse on the left is now the town library. The road beside the school leads over to a very beautiful Baptist church in a setting of rolling fields and gray stone walls, high over the Atlantic Ocean. Dating to the seventeenth century, it is the oldest Indian Baptist church in North America. The town's police department and town hall are across from the library on the main road.

Gay Head Cliffs and Lighthouse

There are ample parking areas and gift and food shops at the cliffs, which are one of the island's great scenic attractions. Named by British sailors in the seventeenth century, the cliffs were often mentioned in logs and journals. They were a landmark to sailors outward bound on voyages that sometimes lasted years, and for those returning to New Bedford or the Vineyard, they were the first sight of home. The twisted strata of these multicolored cliffs, which are of particular interest to geologists and paleontologists, recount millions of years of the earth's formation. Years ago the Indians dug clay out of the cliffs to be shipped to mainland potteries on coastal schooners. Facing west from the lookout, the Elizabeth Islands, on your right, extend in a chain from Woods Hole, and the small deserted island of Noman's Land is to your left.

As early as 1799 there was a tended lighthouse on this point to mark the entrance to Vineyard Sound and to warn ships away from the great reef of glacial boulders extending out from the cliffs for almost a mile. It was here on the night of January 18, 1884, that the worst shipwreck in Martha's Vineyard history occurred when the ironhulled steamship, *The City of Columbus,* struck the rocks. En route from Boston to Savannah on a bright moonlit night, with heavy seas running and high winds, the vessel struck the ledge about 3:00 A.M. It was five hours before a Humane Society boat was able to reach the vessel, where survivors clung to the icy rigging in the frigid blackness, praying and waiting for dawn. The strength of 122 passengers, one after another, gave out, and they dropped into the sea. The heroic efforts of the islanders who rowed through mountainous waves to rescue survivors is another memorable episode in the history of Gay Head's mariners, most of whom were Indian.

The original lighthouse here was one of the first revolving ones in the country; often the wooden works became swollen in damp weather, and the keeper or his wife was obliged to turn the light by hand all night long. In 1856 this was replaced by a larger steel structure that housed a stronger light with a Fresnel lens. In 1952 the present automatic light was erected, and the old lens was given to the Vineyard Museum.

Noman's Land Island

Although there have been many theories, the origin of the name of Noman's Land is unknown. In the nineteenth century this was a fishing outpost for Vineyarders who built fish houses on the north side of the island and spent half the year here, cod fishing spring and fall and lobstering in summer. Some brought their families with them, others went back and forth to the Vineyard, and a few families lived here year-round, fishing and raising sheep. In the late 1800s as many as sixty boats worked out of Noman's Land. It is now owned by the United States government and is used for naval bombing practice, although conservationists are hopeful it will one day become a wildlife preserve.

Moshup's Trail

Facing Down-Island from the cliffs, Moshup's Trail is to your right. The road loops down along the Gay Head beach and then connects back to the South Road. The Indians called Gay Head Aquinnah, meaning "Long End" or "Point," and Moshup's Trail is named for a legendary giant and hero of both the Vineyard and Cape Cod Indians. Among the many stories about his extraordinary abilities is one about the boulders at Devil's Bridge, which he is supposed to have put down so he could walk over to Cuttyhunk at the tip of the Elizabeth Islands; as the legend goes, he abandoned the idea before it was completed. He is also said to have dragged his toe over a barrier beach that connected Noman's Land and the Vineyard, causing the beach to disappear with the first high tide. His most famous feat, according to Indian lore, was to knock the ashes out of his pipe while fishing off Chappaquiddick, thereby making Nantucket.

Lobsterville

Again facing Down-Island from the Cliffs, go left on Lighthouse Road, which makes a loop down along Vineyard Sound to Lobsterville. This was the island's most important fishing village in the nineteenth century before the creek leading into Menemsha Pond was dredged and riprapped in 1905 to make Menemsha Harbor. The cluster of net houses and fish houses used by lobstermen, trap fishermen, and hand-liners in the days when smacks arrived from New York to buy lobsters for five cents apiece is gone. It is a fine beach for swimming and fishing. The Cranberry Lands across the road is a nesting site for thousands of gulls in the early spring and a favorite spot for bird watchers. There is no trespassing allowed on these beautiful, low, rolling moors covered with wild roses, bayberry, dusty miller, and cranberries.

At the end of the Lobsterville Road is a boat ramp, and just across the creek is Menemsha. To get there, retrace your steps back to Lighthouse Road and South Road, and go left to Beetelebung Corner.

Middle Road

At the intersection of Middle and South roads at Beetlebung Corner, a short trip straight ahead leads to a view of a beef cattle farm with open, rolling fields and a wide sweep of the blue Atlantic Ocean beyond. Two miles past the farm, the first tarred road on the left goes up a steep hill to Peaked Hill, one of the highest points on the island, 298 feet above sea level. This panorama of the Atlantic Ocean, Elizabeth Islands, Menemsha Pond, and the high, rolling Chilmark hills gives a bird's-eye view of the island's extraordinarily varied terrain. A signal corps detachment was stationed here during World War II when military installations were hurriedly erected on both the Vineyard and Nantucket.

Menemsha

Return to Beetlebung Corner and bear right on the Menemsha Cross Road, which leads down to Chilmark's port, considered to be the last true fishing village on the island. The large number of pleasure boats tied up here each summer has somewhat changed the character of the port, however.

Menemsha has its own post office in the general store, and the fishers' colorful boathouses lining the west side of the basin have been a favorite subject of artists for years. The island's Coast Guard station is located here, and their vessels are kept on this side of the harbor; the commercial fishing boats tie up along Dutcher's Dock on the east side of the basin. Menemsha now has a marina with plug-ins, and tourism dominates the local economy.

Menemsha Bight, just offshore, and the sea around Noman's Land have always been popular sport-fishing areas, and charter boats go out from here to the fishing grounds. The beach is open to the public.

The Baptist church in Gay Head is the oldest Indian Baptist church in North America. (left)

The Mill Pond in West Tisbury is a fun place to feed the ducks and swans. (top)

The Gay Head Cliffs are a premier tourist attraction on the island. (bottom)

Built in 1769, Tashmoo Farm, with its rolling hills framed by stone walls, is one of the most beautiful on the island.

North Tisbury

Leaving Menemsha, take the North Road to North Tisbury. There are no easily identifiable historic sites along this wooded, winding road, which, like the South Road, is inland from the sea. The dirt driveways you see along the way lead to private houses whose occupants value their privacy and the seclusion of the North Shore.

On the right you will pass the sign for Tea Lane, which dates back to Revolutionary times when no true patriot would drink tea that had been taxed by England but would smuggle it in "duty free." A Captain Robert Hillman sneaked some tea home from England for a sick relative and gave the little dirt road its name.

There are several brooks along the North Road that run down from the Chilmark hills into Vineyard Sound. Years ago they provided sites for a brickyard, where Vineyard clay was used to make bricks for local consumption as well as export, a paint mill, and several gristmills.

Some of the island's famous sea captains came from the North Shore area, including Captain George Fred Tilton and his brother, Captain Zeb Tilton. The former gained renown for his 2,000-mile trek down the coast of Alaska to get help when America's whaling fleet was caught in the ice at Point Barrow in 1897. Zeb, a legendary coastal schooner captain who owned the *Alice S. Wentworth,* was known from Boston to Brooklyn for his wit, skill, and attraction for women during the sixty years he moved freight under canvas.

At a fork in the road, bear left beside the magnificent oak tree with huge branches curving down to the ground. You are in the center of North Tisbury, although, increasingly, people are calling it West Tisbury, which can be a little confusing. At one time the town was an agricultural community. Here were a church, schoolhouse, blacksmith, and general store, where for years the stage from Vineyard Haven changed horses. All have disappeared, but the town has retained its rural charm; there are some interesting old houses and several stores well worth seeing. Stop at Humphrey's Vineyard Food Shop, an island institution, where delicious baked goods, seasonal jellies and jams, and beverages are for sale.

Christiantown

A half mile along State Road, on your left, is the sign for Indian Hill Road. This leads to a crossroads and a sign pointing straight ahead down a dirt road to the Indian graveyard and chapel at Christiantown, which is a half-mile farther. This ancient township was started in 1659 with a grant of one square mile given by Sachem Josias Keteanummin of Takemmy as a new home for Indian converts to Christianity. A plaque on a boulder commemorates "the services of Governor Thomas Mayhew and his descendant missionaries who here labored among the native Indians."

The Christiantown Meeting House, or chapel, was erected in 1829. It is a fascinating little building surrounded by a wildflower garden, and inside there is a tiny altar and six pews on either side of the aisle. The nearby fieldstones mark the old Indian gravesites.

Behind the Indian graveyard a footpath leads through the woods to the fire tower lookout, which commands a view of the surrounding countryside.

Lambert's Cove

Return to the State Road and bear left toward Vineyard Haven. A short distance ahead on the left is Lambert's Cove Road. Inland from the sea, with woods and hills to preclude any view of the water, it is a pretty drive through the countryside, but there are few historic sites visible from the road. Lambert's Cove was once a sizeable fishing and farming community with its own ferry running to Woods Hole. A short distance in from the highway on the right is Uncle Seth's Pond, now a favorite place for ice skating. Farther along you'll pass the Methodist church, which originated in 1846, and its lovely old hillside cemetery. Alongshore in this area there was once a brick works that produced both red and yellow brick from island clay.

Tashmoo Lookout

Lambert's Cove Road dead-ends back on the State Road by the lovely Tashmoo Farm, with its magnificent stone walls and rolling pastures. Bear left, and just ahead on the left is Tashmoo Lookout, a lovely view across Vineyard Sound to the Elizabeth Islands. Tashmoo in Indian dialect means "At the Great Spring." The opening to the Sound was originally a creek where anglers used to seine for herring in the spring. It wasn't until the present century that the opening was dredged and riprapped to enable boats to enter what is now known as Lake Tashmoo.

A short distance ahead is the center of Vineyard Haven, the end of this tour.

Summer residents Betsy and Walter Cronkite leave Edgartown Harbor on their yawl, Wyntje, *for a cruise down to Maine.* (COURTESY WALTER CRONKITE)

EPILOGUE

The fascination of an island resort is that it provides an escape from urban America; it also offers the seclusion, simplicity, easy point of reference, and strong identity of small-town America. On the Vineyard, the magical attraction is not only the individuality of the six towns—the historic villages, the galaxy of entertainment in the Down-Island towns, and the bucolic Up-Island farms—but the variety and scope of the island's natural beauty: the timeless lure of the restless sea framing the broad, windswept beaches; brilliant skies; thick woodlands of scrub oak and pine; freshwater ponds and streams; high, rolling hills reminiscent of Scottish moors; excellent offshore sailing; and harbors teeming with the graceful movement of ships.

The soaring popularity of the island has been both a blessing and a curse. The Vineyard is very fragile, after all, and the delicate balance between people and nature—so necessary for the island to retain its character—is constantly being challenged. Overdevelopment in many areas is threatening this balance, and growth, often without planning, has been the source of endless controversy. It has jeopardized the water table, wildlife, wetlands, harbors, and shellfish industry. Most important of all, the island risks losing its innate personality, that unique quality that offshore islands acquire over the centuries. The great interest in America's heritage has increased dramatically since the Bicentennial, especially on the Vineyard where the thread of history winds through the island like gossamer. Historic roots are the island's most valuable asset.

Fortunately, many dedicated individuals, both summer and island residents, have had the foresight and appreciation for history to understand the problem. They have worked long and hard to set aside wildlife areas and preserve historic buildings, aware that overdevelopment would not only damage the natural environment, but also change the face of the island in an irreversible manner.

Toward this end there are six organizations working to preserve, protect, and acquire properties to help maintain the balance. Currently about 20 percent of the island's land mass, including wetlands, farmland, beaches, and wildlife areas, is protected from any commercial development, and the work goes on. While the island has been settled for 350 years, it belongs to nature and to history, and its future depends on how citizens and visitors treat this beautiful, but very fragile, outpost.

INDEX

E

F

G

Acknowledgments

The author is indebted to the following individuals for their generous assistance in helping to put together this guide: Art Railton, former President of the Vineyard Museum; Richard Reston, Executive Editor/General Manager of the *Vineyard Gazette,* for use of the paper's superb archives; Mike Wallo, Production Manager of the *Gazette,* for his excellent photography; Bruce Markot, Managing Editor of the Globe Pequot Press, for his thoughfulness and expertise; and Mace Lewis, my editor at Globe Pequot, for his help with this edition.

All selections of lodgings and restaurants have been made by the author. *No one can pay or is paid to be in this book.*

About the Author

Polly Burroughs has been a resident of Martha's Vineyard for many years, both in summer and now year-round. She has written ten previous books, including Globe Pequot's *Guide to Nantucket, Zeb: A Celebrated Schooner Life, The Great Ice Ship Bear, Thomas Hart Benton: A Portrait, Eisenstaedt: Martha's Vineyard,* and *Martha's Vineyard Houses and Gardens.*

When she's not writing, Mrs. Burroughs enjoys such island activities as tennis, swimming, and gardening.

About the Photographer

Mike Wallo, a professional photographer for fifteen years, is also the Production Manager of the *Vineyard Gazette.* Originally from New Jersey, he attended Rutgers University and worked for a number of New Jersey daily newspapers before joining the *Gazette* staff in 1980. He and his wife, Susan, and their daughter live in Oak Bluffs.

Most of the photographs shown here have been previously published in the *Vineyard Gazette.*